IRAQ:
Military Victory,
Moral Defeat

Thomas C. Fox

Sheed & Ward

Sheed & Ward™ is a service of National Catholic Reporter Publishing Company, Inc.

Library of Congress Catalog Card Number: 91-61249

ISBN: 1-55612-464-3

Published by: Sheed & Ward
                115 E. Armour Blvd. P.O. Box 419492
                Kansas City, MO 64141-6492

To order, call: (800) 333-7373

To Hoa
and the children,
Daniel, Christine and Catherine

Contents

Foreword

Your brother's blood is crying out to me (Genesis 4:10).

As Christians, we have the obligation to reflect on the events of our time from the perspective of God's will and his Word, which we know from the Scriptures. This reflection becomes all the more urgent in relation to the recent war in the Gulf.

On the one hand, thousands of people were killed (as I write there are no definite figures, but the estimate is more than 100,000). On the other hand, arms and weapons were used that cost billions of dollars. A Third World country has been destroyed by sophisticated First World weapons. And the money used to make these weapons could have been used for health, housing and education in the United States and elsewhere.

The kind of reflection we will be able to make depends on *who* is making it. Will the majority of North American Christians and others take the time to read and meditate on the contents of this book? Or is this book being written only for future generations who will wonder: What type of Christian lived in the United States at the end of the 20th century?

When Martin Luther King, Jr., first started to preach, he launched an appeal to "save the soul of America." As I look at the newspaper pictures of proud desert Arabs kneeling to kiss the boots of adolescent American soldiers, I wonder how this will affect the "anima" of America? Who will step forward now to "save the soul of America"?

The First North-South War

Brazilian Senator Severo Gomes wrote in Sao Paulo's largest newspaper that he doesn't know anyone, even those who supported the war in the Gulf, who believes that the war was waged to liberate Kuwait and to defend liberty and justice. Everyone believes the United States wanted Kuwait's oil and that, to get it, the U.S. government did not hesitate to massacre Iraq. He concludes that it is a case of international robbery.

On the political level, the *National Catholic Reporter* (Feb. 22, 1991) sums up U.S. aims in the Middle East: protection of the flow of oil to the West; containment of the Soviet Union; survival of Israel; support for friendly Arab regimes.

Democracy was not a priority, because, even in Arab countries whose governments support the United States, the majority of poor Arabs resent the power of the United States being used in their area and resent their natural resources being used only in the First World's self-interest.

These economic and political factors show us that the Gulf War is the contradiction of the American dream. Millions of immigrants fled to the United States in the past centuries to escape from endless European wars. They were dreaming of *peace*. They dreamed with the prophet Isaiah (2:4): "He will settle disputes among great nations. They will hammer their swords into plows and their spears into pruning knives. Nations will never again go to war, never prepare for battle again."

When violence becomes a national idol, this is no longer the American dream. The immigrants dreamt of abundance for all and the fullness of life. The Gulf War is a deep denial of this dream. It is the denial of everything that is most essential to the American soul.

Pope John Paul II called the war a cause of great bitterness. In his letter to President Bush, he writes, "We cannot pretend that the use of arms, and especially of today's highly sophisticated weaponry, would not give rise, in addition to suffering and destruction, to new and perhaps worse injustices" (*NCR*, Feb. 1, 1991).

Once again, I want to underline that this appeal of the Holy Father corresponds to the American dream. That it was ignored by the American government is a sign that something is *very* wrong in the United States today.

The immigrants dreamt of having strong and courageous children so that they could build a country based on the ideals of the Constitution. In the voluntary Army of the United States, 35 to 40 percent of the foot soldiers were Afro-Americans. The majority of the soldiers came from underprivileged backgrounds. The sons and daughters of America's urban poor are sent to kill the poor of Iraq, a Third World country. Is this not a violation of the spirit of the American Constitution?

This war, started by the American government in defense of *economic interests*, was a betrayal of the American people.

The people of the United States have proved and continue to prove that they respect and want to promote justice and liberty for the poor of the Third World. All of us in Third World countries have reason to acknowledge the generosity of the American people. For this reason, the use of violence in Grenada and Panama and the unrestrained use of arms in Iraq against the poor of the Third World is an inexplicable contradiction! And it is shameful!

Do 90 percent of the American people really support what the U.S. government did against the poor of Iraq? Or have the government and the media persuaded the majority that that is not what really happened?

History will judge who was "patriotic" in the United States before and during the Gulf War. Was it those who defended the poor in the Third World, or was it those who, despite the price in human lives and lost prestige, wanted to maintain their own wealth and "way of life"?

The American people have no idea of the effect of the Gulf War on Third World countries. Among the Arab countries, the rich sided with the U.S. government while the *millions* of poor condemned this military aggression. In the rest of the Third World, there is hatred and fear: When will they decide to invade us? And what will be the "motive"? Drugs? The foreign debt? The right of every American citizen to enjoy a 75-cent cup of coffee?

Signs for the Future

As a Christian from the Third World, I would like to end this reflection on the Gulf War by quoting some Christians from the First World.

In an interview in the Spanish newspaper *El Pais,* John Kenneth Galbraith stated: "We have to terminate the international commerce in arms; war does not only bring the horror of death to those who lose it, but also to the winners. War is a horror for all involved; we have to deepen our solidarity with the poor of the Third World, especially in the areas of education and culture. No illiterate country is rich and no rich country is illiterate; a new international order can only be based on overcoming the inequalities that cause international conflicts."

This type of declaration should stimulate the birth of a new generation of politicians, scientists, technicians and industrialists who honor the American dream instead of continuing to shame it.

Lutheran Bishop Herbert Chilstrom stated to President Bush: "I believe . . . that unless you bend every effort to avoid war . . . you will be responsible for leading the United States and the world into *one of the darkest chapters of human history"* (*NCR,* Jan. 25, 1991).

I have been told by a few North American Lutheran ministers visiting Brazil that they dare not read the declaration made by a Lutheran bishop in their churches. The media has persuaded good, churchgoing Christians that this is the United States' "shining hour." It is not. The use of this military force comes close to what the Book of Revelation calls idolatry. As Tom Fox wrote in the *National Catholic Reporter,* God is said to have begun the history of the world between the Tigris and Euphrates rivers. President Bush now has set out to imitate him at the same location, going to battle there to begin his new international order!

Ironically, the American government chose January 15, the birthday of Martin Luther King, Jr., as the last day before war would be declared. In honor of this great pacifist, I would like to quote some of his words during the war in Vietnam:

> "I am convinced that if we are to get on the right side of the world revolution, we as a nation must undergo a radical revolution of values. A true revolution of values will soon cause us to question the fairness and justice of many of our past and present policies. A true revolution of values will soon look uneasily on the glaring contrast between poverty and wealth. With righteous indignation, it will look across the seas and see individual capitalists of the West investing huge sums of money in Asia, Africa and South America, only to take the profits out with no concern for the social betterment of the countries, and say: 'This is not just.' It will look at our alliance with the landed gentry of Latin America and say: 'This is not just.' The Western arrogance of feeling that it has everything to teach others and nothing to learn is not just. A true revolution of values will lay hands on the world order and say of war: 'This way of settling differences is not just.' This business of burning human beings . . . of injecting poisonous drugs of hate into the veins of peoples normally humane, of sending men home from dark and bloody battlefields physically handicapped and psychologically deranged, cannot be reconciled with wisdom, justice and love."

Indeed, we may ask again with Martin Luther King, Jr.: Who will save the soul of America?

Cardinal Paulo Evaristo Arns
Sao Paulo, Brazil
April 2, 1991

Acknowledgments

It was not until I sat down to thank those who helped shape this book that I realized how many were involved and over how many years the process occurred.

While the most immediate subject of this book is a war, it is, in a deeper sense, about family, the global family. My vision of this larger family was shaped by my experiences of growing up within my own immediate family. I could never have written this book, for example, without having experienced the faith, love and compassion of my parents, Clement and Alice. Nor could I have attempted it with confidence without the understanding and support I have received over many years from my brothers, Jim and Bob, and sisters, Betty, Mary and Ginny.

Looking back, I can see how much my years in Vietnam have shaped my thinking. I am grateful to International Voluntary Services, which sent me to Vietnam. The IVS leadership was always supportive of my work. Two in particular encouraged me, Don Luce and Gene Stoltzfus. I am grateful to the many Vietnamese I came to know. In particular, I think of my wife's relatives and especially her parents, To Van Ba and Nguyen Thi Nham.

I owe gratitude to those who helped me get started in journalism. While in Vietnam, I first realized the importance of a good editor. Not only did Robert Hoyt, then *NCR* editor, encourage me, he honed my contributions into quality prose. Later in Vietnam, Gloria Emerson at *The New York Times* and Stan Cloud at *Time* offered valuable counsel.

More immediately, I can trace this book back to my arrival at *NCR*. I took over as editor in 1980 from Arthur Jones, now the paper's editor-at-large. It was at his suggestion that I undertook the project to write this book. He recognized its potential value and also, I believe, knew the therapeutic value it would have for its author, so upset by what was occurring in the Middle East.

I cleared my office desk, having received the blessing of *NCR* Publisher Bill McSweeney. That took me to my home word processor, behind which I disappeared until the writing was done. I sent my first drafts electronically to Jones, who edited them and offered suggestions for the second drafts. My assistant, Jean Blake, meanwhile, became crucial to the process. She was the central electronic relay, working modems and passwords with all the hectic ease required of the beasts. She was crucial to the process and I owe her special thanks. *NCR* copy editor Candie Sackuvich took my revised drafts and copy edited them. They, in turn, were scrutinized by Sheed & Ward production editor Andy Apathy and production assistant Francis Tilton. I am grateful for the care they brought to their work.

The entire newsroom staff, Michael Farrell, Dawn Gibeau, Tim McCarthy, Pat Windsor, Demetria Martinez and Chris Curry, shaped this book by their work and coverage during the Gulf War. They took on extra loads when I was working at home. I am also grateful to the *NCR* Washington Bureau, including Bureau Chief Joe Feuerherd, Dorothy Vidulich, Evan Gahr and Jones, as I am to Vatican Affairs Writer Peter Hebblethwaite. He kept us abreast with sound analysis of Vatican policy as it pertained to the Middle East during the war.

I want also to acknowledge George E. Irani, a Lebanese-born American and professor of political science at Franklin College. His understanding of the Middle East helped me enormously.

NCR contributors Bill Kenkelen and Patricia Lefevere gathered information from the West Coast and the New York area, respectively. Steve Askin and Carole Collins kept a special watch on the press, keeping me abreast of Gulf-related news not appearing on the general wire services. I owe sincere thanks to these and many other contributors and stringers throughout the U.S.

Finally, I want to thank my wife, Hoa, for her moral and practical support, including the many appreciated glasses of fruit juice she provided while I was at the word processor.

Introduction

This is a book about war and human failure.

Paradoxically, it is a hopeful book because through the description of one newspaper's coverage of the war with Iraq it depicts the journeys of many people who increasingly reject modern warfare, multibillion-dollar arms sales and the tragic waste of nuclear stockpiling. These people envision a more peaceful world and are mapping out ways to realize that vision.

The book is written with several audiences in mind, no one more important than the others.

First, it is written for those who protested U.S. policies in the Persian Gulf. For months, they felt deep sadness. As much of the rest of the nation rushed to embrace the war, they felt lonely and, at times, questioned their values and even the soundness of their minds. My hope is that this book will comfort them, they will be relieved to learn they were not alone, they were not "crazy," and that many others, in the United States and abroad, felt and thought as they did.

Next, this book is written for those many Americans who went along with the war while quietly harboring serious reservations about its morality. Many of these people simply did not have the information to explore their concerns, nor the words to articulate them. They felt relief when the war was over, but continued to doubt the process that led this country to war. They are deeply saddened by the death and suffering their nation unleashed upon the Iraqi people, including, in the war's rippling aftermath, the Kurdish minority along Iraq's borders with Turkey and Iran. "Surely," they might be saying to themselves, "there must be another way." This book describes that other way.

Finally, the book is written for those who gave their unconditional support to "Desert Storm." Maybe they had a relative or friend ordered into the Middle East. Maybe they felt U.S. actions were not only justified but absolutely required. For these people, this book is written as a challenge. It is meant to question, not to condemn. It is meant to explain another viewpoint.

This book tells at least four stories. The first one is mine—the story of a civilian volunteer-turned-journalist in Vietnam. It is grounded in the Vietnam War and the sufferings of Vietnamese refugees. Journalism led me to the *National Catholic Reporter*, as its editor, and, a quarter century after Vietnam, to *NCR*'s coverage of the Gulf War.

Next, the book is the story of some faith-inspired Americans who have dedicated their lives—some taking many personal risks—to building a more just and peaceful world order. Thirdly, the book describes the way *NCR* covered those attempts toward peace and justice from the mid-1960s on.

Finally, it is the story of this newspaper's alternative coverage of the Gulf War. In addition, the Appendix contains a sampling of articles and commentaries which appeared in *NCR* during the course of the war. Woven together, these stories and articles explore the moral issues and questions that were trampled over during this country's heedless rush into a tragic and unnecessary war.

Tom Fox
Roeland Park, Kansas
April 1991

1

From Vietnam to Iraq

Many times I said to family, friends and colleagues at the *National Catholic Reporter*, where I am editor, that it would never come to war. No way would there be a Middle East war. No way would diplomacy fail. No way would the Bush administration consciously choose modern warfare, aware of its terrifying consequences, both known and unforeseen. Not in 1991. We had learned too much to believe war would settle anything. Didn't Vietnam teach us that? And given the predictable cost in human lives, irreversible environmental damage and potentially fatal burdens to an already dangerously weakened U.S. economy, certainly the American public would not tolerate another war. Or so I thought. I was wrong.

One morning, cup of coffee in hand, I stood in the *Reporter's* Kansas City, Missouri, newsroom and even bet one editor a dollar it would never come to war. Though I consistently wrote editorials warning of the grave risks of a Middle East war, I privately believed it would never happen. It just couldn't.

Then came the January 16 awakening. That evening I was attending my son, Daniel's, wrestling match at Bishop Miege High School in Roeland Park, Kansas, a few blocks from our home. It was just after 6:00 p.m. A man two rows behind me on the wooden bleachers in the gym, portable radio in his hand, earphone in his ear, blurted out the words: "They're bombing Baghdad." I stood up, my legs wobbled. I was stunned and speechless, my face flushed, my eyes were already wet. I wanted out. I had to get home as quickly as possible to break out of my sudden loneliness, my confusion and anger. More than anything, I wanted to be with my wife, Hoa, in these dreadful, unbelievable moments. Together we had witnessed war before, lived through it, knew it close up, smelled the napalm burns on children's skin, looked into their parents' eyes, visited My Lai, spoke with relatives of the survivors. We had seen the killings and consequences close up. One of our close friends, a student, assassinated another, a father of three. We attended his funeral. Held his wife's hand. God, no! God, no, I thought, not another war!

Hoa and I met in Vietnam. We married in Can Tho, a Mekong Delta town, in a Catholic ceremony on Jan. 16, 1971. Now, 20 years later to the day, our 20th wedding anniversary, there would be no toasts, cheers or smiles. Only prayers and tears over the outbreak of yet another war. Like so many others that first night of the war, we sat before the television, we paced about the house, we were riveted to those early CNN broadcasts from Baghdad. We heard CNN anchorman Bernard Shaw exclaim, "Ladies and gentlemen, I've never been there, but it feels like we're in the center of hell."

The next day I was to write in *NCR*, as the *National Catholic Reporter* is known: "This night, that hell was a U.S. creation."

It is odd, sad, to think about wars as definitional moments. But it is so. And as the Iraq war became the definitional moment in the Bush presidency, it was hammered home to me yet again how much Vietnam was my definitional moment. In what follows in this chapter, my road from Vietnam to Iraq is laid bare for a purpose: to show what went into the way a U.S.-based Catholic newspaper tried to cover and comment on a war that took a nation by surprise. The description of my and Hoa's Vietnam years together is meant to reveal the difficulties besetting Christians who attempt to be pacifistic, nonviolent people in the midst of a war. It would have bearings years later during the U.S.-led war against Iraq.

From the outset, it was clear that the United States public would be blindfolded where the Gulf War was concerned. We had seen the system rehearsed in Grenada and practiced in Panama. This was to be war without death. War without corpses. War without blood spilled, bones broken, eyes blinded, minds shattered. How rightly the commanders referred to the "war theater." Theater was what we would get.

But what was my responsibility as editor of one of the few independent journals in the United States? What could we report? What could we say? Finally, what lessons would I be learning that, set down here, might help like-minded Christians when this country's next quickie, blindfolded war came upon us? My personal frame of reference had to be Vietnam. I was in Vietnam several times, the longest stays from June 1966 to June 1968 and from June 1970 to December 1972. The first time I was there as a volunteer for a nonprofit organization, working with war refugees. I did some occasional free-lance writing then, some for the founding editor of *NCR*, Robert Hoyt. I returned to Vietnam briefly in the summer of 1969 to lead a congressional and interfaith fact-finding team investigating the war, and then in 1970 I went back as a full-time, free-lance journalist writing for *The New York Times* and *Time* magazine.

Hoa had been raised a Buddhist, but, with her family, she converted to Catholicism when she was still at a young age. She attended some forward-thinking Catholic schools and was encouraged by some Catholic nuns to choose a career of service to others. When we first began to get acquainted, she was a social worker in a halfway home for war-injured children, including paraplegics. The house was sponsored by the U.S.-based Committee of Responsibility, a nonprofit organization that offered medical assistance otherwise unavailable in Vietnam to these children. COR, as it was called, functioned through the voluntary efforts of U.S. doctors who were appalled by the war. Volunteers offered their time and raised money to bring the children to the United States for treatment. There were usually at least a half dozen children under Hoa's care, almost all victims of U.S. bombs or artillery. How I came then to hate bombs. How I would shudder two decades later, when military commanders blithely talked about "carpet bomb-ing" Kuwait and Iraq and the people on the ground. Bombs falling over Iraq were simply cartoon pictures. They were silent puffs on video screens for TV audiences to thrill to as, for instance, $1 mil-lion worth of armaments were dropped on a truck traveling along a desert road to obliterate 10 human beings.

But bombs on the ground are very different from bombs on tele-vision. Back in Vietnam, nearly all the children in Hoa's halfway house were from rural areas. We got to know those children, helped raise them before we had children of our own, heard their stories, worried for their uncertain futures.

I remember Lau, a boy of about 10 whose spinal cord was sev-ered. He was just one victim in one central Vietnam act of vio-lence, in just one of hundreds of such battles in that region. It took him years of rehabilitation, some of it in the United States, where he was fitted for braces and learned to walk with them. Eventu-ally, Hoa took Lau back to his village, an event so unusual it was photographed by *Life* magazine photographer Larry Burrows, who later died in a helicopter crash over Laos. I was with Larry the day he died, only in another helicopter. Twenty years ago, journalists could at least offer visions of the hell contained in the phrase "war is hell." Back in that village, the children teased Lau, poked at him. Eventually, he could not make it in his village and returned to Sai-gon, where he lived until the end of the war. We lost touch with Lau after the war, but his condition could not have been helped by the vengeful U.S.-sponsored economic boycott that included medi-cal aid and has continued for more than 15 years. The U.S. govern-ment has kept the World Bank and International Monetary Fund from providing any aid to Vietnam to assist in its painful postwar recovery efforts.

Some other children's stories we never heard in full. All we knew of Vo Tanh was that he had been playing with an explosive device when it blew up in his hands, riddling his face, chest and arms with metal fragments. Now, deaf, mute, blind and missing one hand, he was living with Hoa. He lived in a world of darkness and isolation. Only through touch, by feeling out faces, could he know who was with him. He smiled his acknowledgments of familiarity. I remember holding the stump that was his arm and cursing the war.

I had arrived in Vietnam in the summer of 1966, just after graduating from Stanford University, as a volunteer for the International Voluntary Services, based in Washington, D.C. I would end up living in Vietnam for most of the years between 1966 and 1972. During the first two years, I lived and worked in the Central Vietnam coastal city of Tuy Hoa, the capital of Phu Yen province. In 1966, nearly the entire province was considered to be in the hands of the communist Viet Cong—except for Tuy Hoa. I wore the peasant black pajamas, traveled on a blue Lambretta and never touched a gun.

Those were formative years, defining moments. They also saw my first fumbling efforts in journalism. The *National Catholic Reporter* had been launched some 20 months earlier in Kansas City, Missouri. Michael Novak, then still a progressive, was teaching religious studies at Stanford alongside another Stanford professor, ecumenist Robert McAfee Brown. Novak encouraged me to contact Robert Hoyt, *NCR*'s editor, to let him know I might be available to do some reporting in Vietnam. Hoyt jumped at the chance and became my first editor, also my initial source of encouragement to record my Vietnam experiences.

From day one in Vietnam I began intensive language training. Within six months, I was able to carry on simple conversations with the Vietnamese refugees with whom I was working. Language, I learned then, is the most important gateway to understanding a foreign culture. There were always only two kinds of Americans in Vietnam—those who spoke Vietnamese and those who did not. By speaking the language, one could enter Vietnamese lives, Vietnamese culture, share Vietnamese humor, Vietnamese sorrow. The Vietnamese were infinitely patient with those of us who made the effort to speak their language. Making that effort, in the eyes of the Vietnamese, was a sign of respect for their way of life, an acknowledgment that one was willing to deal with them on an equal footing, unlike most of the colonial and distant French or the arrogant and prejudiced Americans they had known.

There were relatively few of us, most working for church-sponsored organizations, young and idealistic, who tried to live as "Vietnamese" as best we could, eating native foods, living in modest dwellings, working from within the Vietnamese economy. As an IVS volunteer, I was encouraged to listen first and to find out what might be wanted of me before offering help. Initially, my work consisted of finding children with cleft palates among the local population. There were many, apparently as a result of malnutrition among pregnant women or chemical toxins in the environment. I brought the children and their parents to a local hospital where a Korean medical team performed corrective surgery. Within several months the Koreans had changed the faces of close to 100 young children. Later, I became involved in food distribution. It often took weeks, even months, to get small amounts of rice to refugees. The Vietnamese government showed no interest in helping them; indeed the government considered the thousands of refugees living on the sand in camps along the South China Sea as nuisances at best or communist sympathizers at worst. Often I would plead to have rice or cloth shipped from Saigon only to see it sold by the local province chief, a Vietnamese army colonel, on the black market. When I complained to the American advisers stationed in Tuy Hoa, the response was generally the same: "Don't rock the boat."

Meanwhile, it did not take long to realize how senseless it was to think that anyone could "win" the war, or how tragic this war was to Vietnamese society. Beyond all the hundreds of thousands of people being wounded or killed yearly, beyond the millions of refugees being generated, beyond the billions of dollars being spent, the megatons of bombs being dropped were tearing apart the fabric of traditional Vietnamese society. As farmers were forced off their lands, a generation of young men were losing vital rice-planting skills. The rhythms and rituals of food itself were being lost, after centuries. Women were losing their husbands, women who would find their only employment shining shoes or washing linen on U.S. military bases. Young girls, some only 14 years old, were taking up prostitution. It was as substantial a break in social habits and culture as could be imagined in this traditional society.

The United States, meanwhile, was in a war it could never win. Even the staunchest Vietnamese anticommunists—those Vietnamese Catholics the U.S. Navy had brought down from northern Vietnam in 1954 to form the bulwark of the Saigon government and a new South Vietnam—would, in private conversation, often admit the United States was following a hopeless cause. Why hopeless? Because beneath the whole worldview from which Washington conducted the war—using the "communist—anticommunist" scenario—something much deeper was at work: Vietnamese nationalism.

Two decades later, as the United States decided on bombs, not sanctions, to halt an unprincipled dictator, Iraq's Saddam Hussein, the United States would again blithely enter a war with a simplistic "good guys—bad guys" script in hand. Even now, as these words are written, the full extent of the reverberations of the Gulf War in the Arab and Muslim and Middle Eastern communities is far from clear. But the reverberations will be both deep and lasting. One thing history will show us, as the U.S. defeat in Vietnam did, is that as Americans we never factor culture—other people's histories, stories, practices and religion—into our understanding. It is possible to battle and lose the war; it is also possible, as the Gulf War's fallout may yet show us, to win the war and make enemies of our friends.

Vietnamese nationalism was a force that would eventually carry history. But to understand it, one first had to know and appreciate Vietnamese history, never much a U.S. government interest. (Pan-Arabism and Pan-Islamism are forces that eventually will carry history in the Middle East region, but to appreciate that we would first have to understand it.) To study Vietnamese history, to listen to Vietnamese talk about themselves, to read Vietnamese poetry, was to nurture a sense of Vietnamese nationalism. One Vietnamese song put it this way: "One thousand years against the Chinese. One hundred years against the French. Thirty years of civil war." The message was: the nationalists will prevail. (Many Arabs and Muslims may be quietly humming variations on that song in the tea shops and bazaars from Amman to Basra, from Cairo to Brunei.) Even many Vietnamese who benefited from a continued U.S. commitment often expressed pride in the way the North Vietnamese and their allied Viet Cong were carrying on the war against the "foreigners." For the Middle Easterner, read "infidel."

The key to understanding the outcome of the Vietnam War was, then, a knowledge of Vietnamese history. Over the centuries, it was always those Vietnamese who fought against the occupying powers who entered the nation's songs and poems and stirred patriotic pride. Collaborators, by contrast, have been viewed as traitors to the nation. And so the tragedy and futility of the war grew clearer: As soon as President Lyndon Johnson decided to send U.S. ground troops to Vietnam in 1965—ten years before the fall of Saigon—the war was lost. Tens years of killing, ten years of destruction, ten years of "free fire" zones, ten years of napalmed children, ten years of minor and major My Lai's, ten years of B-52 bombings. All of it, every year of it, tragic and futile.

Those were lonely years. During the periods that I was back in the United States with this knowledge, it was tortuous; I felt compelled to travel widely and speak out against the war. Not that all the protesters wanted to hear about the complexities of Vietnam, though many did. Yes, many decent Vietnamese feared the communists and wanted the Americans there. And, yes, many villagers in the South feared the Northern armies and were openly anticommunist. Some protesters, driven more by ideology than a hunger for understanding, feared that such information might prolong the war. However, most I found cared passionately, and their efforts were essential in finally gaining the ear of the U.S. public and turning that public against the war.

But talking about the war was not enough. Eventually, I decided it would be more effective to return to Vietnam, to serve as a kind of personal witness and to report the war and its effects on the people. Information about what was going on in Vietnam had to get back to the United States, where, I felt, people had to rise up and demand that the conflict end. So, after leaving IVS in 1968 and finishing a graduate degree at Yale in Southeast Asian studies, my interest in journalism became focused and directed.

Now, more than 20 years later, what do the readers read in the *National Catholic Reporter* under my editorship? What are we offering them? Not "objective" journalism—I never have believed there is such a thing. Journalists are required to be fair, sensitive and responsible for what they write—but none of us is objective. All journalism is subjective, though some publications prefer to deny it. *The New York Times, The Wall Street Journal, The Washington Post* are great newspapers, provide invaluable information and analysis, but they do so only through certain values and from a largely U.S. corporate viewpoint. They may not see it that way, but it is so. They are not "objective." Many European newspapers are published by political or labor parties. They look at the news from different perspectives, but they are not "objective," either. What matters in the United States, where there are no major, noncorporately financed newspapers or broadcast networks—is that we often end up lacking essential skills of self-criticism. We often end up not being able to see ourselves working and living within powerful institutions. We end up often without the ability to see ourselves as others, in other parts of the world, see us. Were we able to see ourselves in such a manner, we would be moving toward a more "objective" picture of who we really are. Our public information is largely generated from and through one perspective, the U.S. corporate and institutional perspective. There is nothing essentially wrong with such a perspective except when it monopolizes information. Then it becomes more than wrong; it becomes dangerous.

The 50,000-circulation *National Catholic Reporter* is, at its best, one publication among a handful of other national publications that attempts to an alternative perspective. And what, in a constantly tumultuous, perennially unjust world, is our perspective? What, when war breaks out, as it did January 16, 1991, are the critical viewpoints that readers may not be gaining elsewhere? Such are the questions that have shaped *NCR* since its beginnings, from the Vietnam War to the Gulf War.

During my Vietnam days, I was graced with a clear perspective from which to report. I remember vividly the visit of about a dozen Vietnamese refugees, all men, some in frayed shirts and pants, others in peasant black pajamas, to my one-room, cinderblock house in Tuy Hoa. Apparently, they had been watching me work in and around the Ninh Tinh refugee camp for some time, saw me struggling to learn their language, apparently thought I could be trusted and finally decided to take me into their confidence, a rare occurrence between rural Vietnamese and Americans during the war years. Variously squatting and sitting in a circle, they said they came to talk about my work. They smoked some cigarettes, drank some tea I offered them, and eventually got around to what they wanted to say. Their message was quite simple: "If you want to help us, then tell your people what they are doing to our country. Tell them about the war." I believe I understood then that my alternate perspective would be to interpret events from the view of the people at the bottom, to report what was happening to those least likely to be heard—but most likely to suffer—in a tumultuous, in this case, a war-torn world. In our editorial offices, we call it "reporting from the bottom up rather than from the top down."

As Iraq viciously violated Kuwait—itself no great model of a decent society—memories of those refugees, the reality of the need to report and comment on the war from the perspective of everyday people, became paramount.

Meanwhile, there were two other currents under way in my life that would also influence the way *NCR* went about its Gulf War coverage. The first was my 20-year journey toward pacifism, and the second was the implanting in my psyche of an appreciation of how totally negating war is. It is the ultimate slap in the face of creation—and the Creator itself. Bear with me briefly as together we trace these two facets as they became more vital to my makeup as an editor—for they dramatically influence my worldview and serve a distinct purpose as we look ahead to assess and apply the lessons from the 43-day Gulf War.

Although long in coming, I can now say that I am a Catholic pacifist. Or, at least, would like to be considered one. I see pacifism more as an ideal to be achieved than a state of being. The word *pacifist* rarely does justice to the idea of pacifism. It wrongly conjures up the image of a kind of passive withdrawal. As a result, many pacifists avoid the term, preferring to speak of active nonviolence or simply living nonviolently. Pacifism is anything but passive. In a world so characterized by violence, pacifists counter contemporary currents, currents of violence so pervasive it becomes a struggle even to explain the meaning of nonviolence, let alone live it.

My belief in the fundamental truth of nonviolence has been evolving slowly over the years. It is not too much to say that Vietnam took me to the threshold of pacifism, and Iraq led me to step over it. Nonviolence, I believe, represents the most hopeful long-term path for the establishment of a just and peaceful world. It is a path that speaks a truth about human existence. And as I have grown to realize this, my Christian faith—the belief that Jesus spoke the truth and taught nonviolence—has deepened as well. He said, "You have heard that it was said, 'Love your friends, hate your enemies.' But now I tell you: Love your enemies and pray for those who persecute you" (Matthew 5:43-44).

My journey to gaining an appreciation for nonviolence as a way of life goes back to my college years at Stanford University. I had grown up in a Catholic family in which the subject of pacifism was never mentioned. The faith of my Polish mother, Alice, was as solid as it was pious; Tuesday evenings it was off to St. Sebastian Church for devotions to Our Mother of Perpetual Help. Our family was large (two brothers, three sisters) and there was always something to petition. Like many of his generation, my father, Clement, a neuroanatomist at Marquette University Medical School, considered himself a *Commonweal* Catholic. He was open-minded, progressive, and he cultivated the intellectual component of his faith. My father counted many Jesuits among his close friends, and he had a great admiration for Monsignor Ronald Knox, whose translation of the New Testament was like poetry to his ears. I attended Marquette High School in the early 1960s; I vaguely remember thinking about war then and being introduced to "just-war" theory. In those years, part of being a Catholic, it seemed, was having to fight, if necessary, for one's faith. Faith, then, was more or less synonymous with country. There was no reason to think otherwise. During my freshman year at Stanford, I stumbled across a group of pacifists, some students, others poets and writers—visitors to the university. The dean of freshmen, Dwight Clark, was a Quaker. He was the first person to share with me the principles of nonviolence. He started with the simplest of ideas, the notion that violence leads to further violence. A quarter century later, I would be placing those words in editorials warning our nation not to use military force in the Persian Gulf.

At Stanford I was attracted to what for me were new ideas—new, at least, in the comprehensive way they were being presented. I remember quietly lamenting at the time that my own faith did not stress what seemed to be so authentic and sane an approach to life. It was as if these people were more peace-loving than the one I had learned to call the Prince of Peace. This deeply troubled me. Making it worse, these San Francisco poets insisted they were atheists. I had never met a professed atheist before. And here they were arguing that organized religion and the very idea of God through history had been the cause of much of the world's violence and wars. Those were difficult months for me, but they represented my first efforts to sort out my faith for myself. Much of what they were saying made sense to me but was at conflict with my religion, at least my religion as I had understood it at the time. Was this to be the fulfillment of earlier warnings from some of my high-school teachers—warnings dismissed by my father at the time—that if I attended a "non-Catholic" college I could risk losing my faith?

I came to know a Catholic priest, a university chaplain named Father John S. Duryea, a towering man and pastor. He was wonderfully alive in the world of ideas. I began to attend Mass at St. Ann's chapel in Palo Alto, where he celebrated Mass daily. I remember his spectacular sermons and the way they attracted the students, faculty, Catholics and others from throughout the area. Duryea was cut from the mold of the great California naturalist John Muir. He loved the outdoors and enjoyed nothing more than hiking with students in Yosemite National Park, where he would talk endlessly about the beauty of creation and God's mysterious ways. He said God spoke to him through the clouds and the mountains and the flowers that grew along the paths we walked together.

Duryea sensed that I was troubled. We talked and he suggested that I start reading the writings of a Trappist monk named Thomas Merton. One of the books I purchased was *A Thomas Merton Reader*. It opened my imagination and mind to whole new vistas of my faith. Here was a man who saw Jesus not only as a loving and compassionate person, but also as one committed to nonviolence as a way of life. More important, Merton was saying that Catholics needed to rediscover the nonviolence essential to what Jesus had taught and reintroduce it into our lives and church. In Merton I found a contemporary Catholic thinker who had wrestled with some of the very notions I was then trying to sort out. Merton opened me to paradox and contradiction and risk-taking as essential components of the Christian faith. He showed me that peace comes only by way of a radical discontent with the world as it is. This Trappist was a Catholic idealist even before the idealism of

the 1960s, which was also shaping me. I was attracted to his notions of contemplation and its relevance to the issues of the day. In
silence, he found truth. In isolation, he found involvement and answers to the ills of the world. Merton became a spiritual friend. I
found many elements of my own faith, my struggles, my longings,
my efforts to respond to new questions of early adulthood in this
one man. Merton later wrote in *New Seeds of Contemplation*:

> When I pray for peace I pray God to pacify not only the
> Russians and the Chinese but above all my own nation and
> myself. When I pray for peace I pray to be protected not
> only from the Reds but also from the folly and blindness of
> my own country. When I pray for peace, I pray not only
> that the enemies of my country may cease to want war, but
> above all that my own country will cease to do the things
> that make war inevitable. In other words, when I pray for
> peace I am not just praying that the Russians will give up
> without struggle and let us have our own way. I am pray-
> ing that both we and the Russians may somehow be re-
> stored to sanity and learn how to work out our problems as
> best we can, together, instead of preparing for global sui-
> cide.

I could relate to that. Years later, as our nation rushed forward
into a war against Iraq, Merton's words returned to me. Though he
had written them years earlier, his words spoke to the void of in-
trospection I was sensing throughout the American public and U.S.
media. Merton had something to say to us all. He was among the
first to advise me to view the world in a new and inclusive way.

As Stanford gave me a chance to get acquainted with the spirituality and theory of nonviolence, Vietnam would become the university of practical knowledge. In retrospect, I see that Vietnam
was a triple blessing for me: first, for providing the opportunity to
meet my wife, Hoa; second, for providing the chance to see life
and our nation through the eyes of another culture; and third, for
providing the chance to associate and identify with victimized people. These three blessings have shaped my values and views of life.

Having lived a portion of my life in the East, and having married an Asian woman, I feel that I can look at the world from a perspective "beyond nationalism." It is a perspective both demanded of Christians and required of the whole human family if we are to live in peace in the 21st century and foster an ecologically sound world. Raised "beyond nationalism," I hope our three children truly are among the first of many generations to experience "world family" understood in a new way.

Seen in this light, I can say those years in Vietnam from 1966 to 1972 were a special gift from God—a gift that carries, I have felt, some reciprocal responsibilities on my part. During my years in journalism, I have held to the notion that reporters serve as bridges for understanding. The problem for many journalists in Vietnam was that they did not live there long enough to understand Vietnamese culture. They often viewed the Vietnamese as no more than a kind of backdrop to the central war story. This was a mistake. The Vietnamese, after all, were the story. It was their land and they would ultimately shape it after the fighting ended. I suspect we have made the same mistake in the Middle East. Hundreds of thousands of Americans passed through the Middle East just as they passed through Vietnam—without seeing it. In Vietnam, at least some Americans—mostly volunteers working for nonprofit relief organizations—had made the effort to live as civilians among the Vietnamese of the countryside, where the farmers carried the greatest burdens of the war.

I worked in the Dong Tac and Ninh Tinh refugee camps, nothing more than tin huts set on sand, the least desirable land, along the coast in Central Vietnam's Phu Yen province. American soldiers said I was crazy for having volunteered to come to Vietnam in the first place, and even crazier for living among the Vietnamese and never carrying a gun. U.S. soldiers, when not on patrol, lived on bases or on compounds surrounded by fences with guards posted at night. I was the peasant in black pajamas. It says much about the preparation U.S. soldiers received in boot camp that many, before coming to Vietnam, were trained to believe black pajamas were the uniforms of the Viet Cong, the South Vietnamese communists. From my experience, speaking the Vietnamese language, eating Vietnamese food, hearing Vietnamese stories, I grew to learn that most Vietnamese saw themselves as having little or no stake in the war. Political allegiances often depended on incidental matters. If a daughter died in an American artillery strike, her family would be supportive of the Viet Cong. If a father was killed by a Viet Cong land-mind explosion, his family would support the South Vietnamese government.

There were some overriding differences, however. To the Vietnamese, the Americans were always the foreigners, frightening people with long noses and blue eyes. They called us "blue-eyed devils" whose weapons were infinitely more destructive than those of the North Vietnamese, not by a count of 10 to one, but sometimes by 10,000 to one. This point is central to understanding the reality of the war and U.S. military involvement in the Third World. It is crucial in terms of understanding Third World perceptions to U.S. force: overwhelming, excessive, indiscriminate, oppressive and demeaning.

The destructive force of modern U.S. weaponry is, of course, categorically different than that of other nations' weapons. This destructive force will be critical, historically, when we finally weigh what the United States actually did in Iraq. It will be critical, too, when others weigh what the United States did and why it set out to do what it did. The Vietnamese have a saying: "When the elephants fight, ants get crushed." In Vietnam—and even more so, a quarter century later in Iraq and Kuwait—only one elephant came to battle. Hundreds of thousands of ants got crushed.

The refugees with whom I lived were forbidden by the U.S. and the South Vietnamese governments to return to their villages. In most cases, their villages were only a one or two day walk from the camp, but they had been largely destroyed in battle or simply declared part of the "free fire zones" that dotted much of the countryside. Anything within these zones was game for patrolling U.S. or Vietnamese helicopter gunships. Many young soldiers hunted from the air with machine guns, shooting at anything that moved. Sometimes they chased hapless peasant farmers or roaming water buffalo. They had the power of gods then, but many returned home haunted by dark nightmares, continuing a life of violence, suffering from post-traumatic stress disorder or committing suicide. We ingest the violence we do to others.

Despite these atrocities, some of the elderly refugees would leave the camps to journey back to their villages to accept their fates. They wanted, they said, to die in their villages and rest among the spirits of their ancestors. I often asked these men and women how peace would one day come to Vietnam. Almost regardless of political preference—and most refugees firmly believed no government was looking after their interests—they would say peace would come to Vietnam only after the Americans returned home. They wanted me to deliver this message to my people.

During those years, I tried a few times to return to life in America. The day I first arrived back in June 1968, I received a notification to report to my draft board for a possible classification change. While I was in Vietnam I had had a draft deferment, but now I was eligible to be reclassified for the draft and entrance into the armed forces. Of course, I knew I would never go. I deeply opposed the war, believed it immoral. When pressed, I would say I felt we were supporting the wrong side. I had nightmares then about the war. Once, I dreamed I was a U.S. soldier protecting a base somewhere in the Vietnamese countryside. North Vietnamese forces began to attack the base. But rather than defending the base, I joined the attackers. My father got upset when I related this dream. He was afraid I was having some kind of breakdown. He said I should see a psychiatrist. A Jewish doctor listened to the story about my stay in Vietnam and said he had no doubt that my mind was healthy, but that I was coping with severe "culture shock."

I told my draft board I opposed the war. They used to tell people who refused induction that they were cowards or did not really understand the war. In my case, their defenses were seriously weakened. I had been in Vietnam, knew what was gong on, had already spent two years there. And, I insisted, I was not afraid to go back. But only as a civilian volunteer.

By then I was publicly speaking out against the war, meeting with the press, talking about the growing refugee problems. When I was only 24, I was viewed as an "expert." That afternoon in Milwaukee, my draft board told me it would work out a deal. It would renew my student deferment, but only if I promised to stop speaking against the war. I told them to forget it. I said I would do everything I could to oppose the senseless war and to denounce it as immoral. That ended the hearing.

I was specifically opposed to the Vietnam War. U.S. laws, however, do not allow for such "selective" objection. They are written to allow those who in conscience oppose all wars to stay out of military service. They are written primarily to allow for wartime exemptions for members of some of the traditional peace churches, such as the Quakers and Mennonites. Even today, U.S. law discriminates against those who, although they may not oppose all wars, use the reasoning of traditional just-war theory to decide they cannot in good conscience participate in a given war.

Several weeks after I met with my draft board, I received a student deferment in the mail. They had apparently decided not to make an issue of my case. Meanwhile, I felt the gap widening between myself, with my opposition to the war, and a seemingly uncaring and apathetic American society that largely supported it. The war did not seem to faze or even interest people then, but I could not stop talking about it. It was a compulsion. I spoke before any audience that would listen: to university students, to high-school classes, to businessmen, to war protesters, to church groups, anyone. I took a master's degree in Southeast Asian studies from Yale University. But I knew I had to return to Vietnam. The irony was that, although it was a very lonely and painful time in my life, only in Vietnam, only in the midst of that war, was I able to be at peace with myself.

The Vietnamese then were much like common-folk Americans, wanting primarily to raise their children, to see them educated and married and to see them have healthy children, too. They wanted to live near family, enjoy life's occasional celebrations, the passages of seasons and life. They wanted to laugh, eat, earn enough money selling rice or vegetables to keep their families intact. Families were everything, but most Vietnamese, try as they might, could not hold them together against the turbulent forces of war and the increasing breakdown of traditional society under the crushing weight of the U.S. military presence.

It took many years, many reports and broadcasts, to wake up the U.S. public to the horrors of Vietnam. The shocking and deplorable My Lai massacre helped to awaken Americans. The fighting in the streets of Saigon during the Tet offensive was instrumental. The photograph of Viet Cong shot dead on a Saigon street by a South Vietnamese colonel also made a difference. Then there was the young girl, naked and running down a road burned by napalm, who finally shocked many Americans into realizing what the war was all about. All of these images helped, along with the growing list of U.S. war dead. Together, they were stirring sensibilities and consciences and creating healthy, natural antiwar feelings.

Years later, this lesson was not lost on the Pentagon, which intentionally began to conduct its wars hidden from the eyes of journalists and their camera lenses. This was to happen most strikingly during the Gulf War. As a result, Americans were denied the images—if not the knowledge—of the agony of the human suffering that constitutes war. This denial is a terrifyingly dangerous development, especially so because Americans proclaim and treasure their constitutional freedoms, including that of a free press. Once during the Gulf War, a camera captured the image of a bird covered with oil from a Persian Gulf oil slick. We saw that bird flapping its wings, struggling in vain to free itself from the polluted Gulf waters. Our hearts felt the pain. We empathized with the helpless creature. Would it live? Would it die? It was so vulnerable. As a result of U.S. military censorship, many of us ended up feeling more empathy for that single bird than for any of the thousands upon thousands of Iraqi men, women and children who were wounded or killed during the bombings of their country. We had completely lost perspective. We had allowed ourselves to be dehumanized.

During the Gulf War we were denied the right to know what our bombs, bought with our money, were doing. And we were denied the right to a clear explanation of why we were doing it. These were issues pressing on us as journalists even before the first bomb dropped, before the word "patriot" was debased into an electronic missile in the American glossary.

It was different for journalists during the Vietnam War. I remember Hoa Da village, October 1967. A regiment of North Vietnamese soldiers entered the village, killed two government officials and prepared for the battle they knew would surely follow. South Vietnamese soldiers quickly surrounded the village, firing on it, but were unable to drive out the enemy. On the second day, U.S. air strikes were called in. The bombardment lasted more than 24 hours. Then a day of silence. As the village smoldered, barely 30 hours after the last air attack, I entered the village to see what had happened and to assess the damage. A U.S. Army major greeted me and called the bombings "a successful effort." Hoa Da was nearly destroyed. He claimed 59 North Vietnamese soldiers died during the bombings. I did not see the bodies. What he did not say—I learned from confused and bitter villagers—was that 52 civilians, mostly the old, the weak and some pregnant women, those unable to flee, had also died.

That is what war does, whether in Southeast Asia or the Middle East. And that is how war-makers and war conductors see their actions.

As I was snapping photographs in Hoa Da, a young man in tattered pajamas came up to me to ask what I planned to do with my film. Before I could finish my answer he snapped: "Be sure to send some pictures to your president!" As he spoke, another man came up to me, two young children holding closely to his legs. He walked up to me, looked directly in my eyes and said: "Your planes killed my grandfather and my nephew." His eyes haunt me to this day. I wrote about Hoa Da (*NCR*, Nov. 27, 1967). It was all I could do.

Bombs are the least discriminating weapons of war. Of all the bombs used in Vietnam, none was more terrifying to the Vietnamese than those from the B-52s, which flew silently at 30,000 feet and let loose a rain of destruction from the heavens. In the spring of 1972, the U.S. Air Force began a particularly ferocious bombing campaign over the Mekong Delta. One afternoon, I visited the Dinh Tuong province hospital and spoke with bombing victims. Most Vietnamese feared to admit being in an area hit with bombs lest they be pegged as Viet Cong sympathizers. Bui Van Si, 58, was an exception. He told me he had been cutting rice one morning with 10 other elderly men when suddenly a B-52 struck. Seconds later, only he and one other man remained alive. "I dived when the bombs began rumbling," he said. "When I got up, eight of the men had simply disappeared."

The United States dropped 4.6 million tons of bombs over Vietnam during the war, one and a half times the tonnage dropped by the allies during World War II. The figures defy human understanding, but precisely because they do, they somehow become more tolerable to the human conscience. This is precisely what happened again during the 43-day war against Iraq, during which the allies dropped 88,000 tons of bombs, the rough equivalent of seven Hiroshima bombs.

I was wrong. I had never believed the United States would go to war over Iraq. But I knew what would happen if it did. In the months from August 1990 to January 1991, I oscillated back and forth between hoping it would not come to war, and knowing what would happen if it did.

These, then, were some of the sentiments and images that influenced my writing and editing of materials presented in *NCR* during the months leading up to the war and during the war itself.

2

Early Warnings

By invading Kuwait, Saddam Hussein caused the world incalculable grief. His unwarranted invasion touched off events leading to the deaths of more than 100,000, perhaps many more. His invasion led to the sufferings of millions, to ecological havoc and to wasted untold billions of dollars. At any point prior to January 16, 1991, Hussein could have started to pull out, prevented a war and still come out a hero in the eyes of his supporters. At any moment, up to and including January 16, 1991, George Bush also could have prevented a war.

Saddam Hussein will not be well remembered in history, at least not in Western history. History's tendency is to side with its own. It will depend largely on who writes the history as to how George Bush will be remembered for his dealings with Iraq.

In August 1990, *NCR* was on its summer schedule, publishing once every two weeks. The invasion of Iraq occurred on press day, obviously too late for that issue. By the time we published our first comments, Iraqi troops had been ransacking Kuwait for two weeks. That intervening period had given us plenty of time to witness the initial Pentagon and Bush administration reactions to Middle East events.

Those reactions should have given us more clues than we allowed, for the reactions in those early days seemingly changed by the hour. They ranged from an initial attitude almost of indifference, to resignation and then to outrage after Bush met with

Britain's hawkish Prime Minister Margaret Thatcher. In retrospect, it appears that Bush was initially *slow* to perceive the political opportunities Saddam Hussein's invasion offered him and was genuinely uncertain about how to react. Thatcher, who had ridden on for more than eight years in office after her Falkland Islands War, may have influenced U.S. history far more than anyone realizes. Whether or not this is so, Bush himself was not "outraged" over Iraq's invasion before his Thatcher visit.

As with all U.S. newspapers facing the Gulf situation, we had to do some quick homework. Not that we had neglected the Middle East. As early as 1984, we sent Steve Askin, then our Washington Bureau chief, to report on growing Israeli-Palestinian tensions. Then in 1988, we tried to tell the same story in a different way. We sent Joe Feuerherd, our Washington correspondent, to Jerusalem to do a series of articles, profiles of Christians, Muslims and Jews working as pathfinders trying to build bridges of understanding among the often hostile communities. Editorially, during both Askin's and Feuerherd's trips, we called for a serious demilitarization of the area and negotiations between the Palestinians and the Israelis. "Christians need to influence U.S. policymakers on a course that encourages demilitarization while addressing Israel's legitimate security needs," we wrote in 1984. "Peace, however, will remain an elusive goal unless just solutions to Palestinian grievances are addressed."

Thus, we had a working familiarity with at least some of the complex and tortuous Middle East problems. Nonetheless, after Iraq's invasion of Kuwait and the beginning of the U.S. military buildup, we decided we needed a larger Middle East map than we'd normally sported in the newsroom in order to identify where the as yet unescalated confrontation was taking place.

"Saddam who? How do you spell 'Hussein'? What's that city again?" we asked as we checked the new map on the wall next to copy editor Candie Sackuvich's desk. We were freshening up our geography as we reviewed the spellings of those Middle East capitals.

By late August, events were moving quickly. For much of our initial information we turned to other newspapers—*The New York Times*, *The Washington Post*—and nightly newscasts. They, in turn, were at the mercy of unnamed U.S. intelligence sources.

What, the world was asking, was Hussein up to? What was happening on the ground in Southern Iraq and Kuwait? What we were told then (and which was later to be disputed by Soviet satellite photographs purchased by and published in the January 6, 1991, edition of the *St. Petersburg Times*) which was that Saddam's forces, having consolidated their hold on Kuwait, were gathering in Southern Kuwait for a possible attack on Saudi Arabia. *The National Catholic Reporter* never attempts to compete with the dailies; that is not a newsweekly's role. We do best with background reporting, analysis and commentary on events. We offer a perspective. But what perspective could we offer on Iraq's invasion of Kuwait? Not much that was different from popular commentary, it seemed. We focused, rather, on what a proper U.S. response might be.

The question going through my mind was how, as editor of a Catholic newspaper, might I reach into the evolving wisdom and values of our church to speak to the moment? And, were there any collective lessons in 26 years of *NCR* that might help? By the time I sat down to write in my office next to the newsroom, U.S. combat troops by the tens of thousands were jetting and sailing to the Persian Gulf.

This was the largest U.S. military movement of its kind, an armada larger than any we saw during the initial stages of the Vietnam War.

About 22 years earlier, Robert Hoyt, founding editor, had sat at his desk in the same building, faced with editorializing about Vietnam. Virtually from the paper's inception in 1964, he and the rest of the *NCR* staff had expressed serious reservations about the wisdom and morality of U.S. intentions in Vietnam. The paper, at the time, probed the moral issues more deeply than virtually any other

U.S. publication, religious or secular. In its January 3, 1968, issue, beneath a headline "You make a desert and call it peace," the paper officially declared its moral opposition to the war. The editorial, in part, says:

> We believe the war in Vietnam is clearly immoral. The commanding reason for this judgment is that the ends for which we are fighting the war cannot be achieved except by nearly total destruction of our enemy in North and South Vietnam. Our government leaders speak constantly of their desire for peace; in fact, however, we are demanding surrender as the price of peace. . . . In short, on the terms of the war as we now define them, we cannot afford to win.

The editorial captured the fundamental illogic of U.S. policy. Vietnam could be pacified only by destroying it. To win would be to lose. Although *NCR*'s response to the Vietnam War helped shape the paper and give it direction, the editors' most lasting moral judgments took years to shape. Unlike that war, which lasted at least a decade, the Gulf War lasted little more than a month. During the Gulf War we had less time to think, but during the Vietnam War the editorial writers, in one sense, had less to draw on: By the time the Gulf War began, there was a considerable body of Catholic opinion and teaching regarding modern warfare that was of recent origin. *NCR*'s 1968 editorial conclusion was bold and well-reasoned, and yet, looking back, it seems tentative given much of the Catholic thinking on war today. In 1968, the Catholic church was still struggling to digest the meaning of the Second Vatican Council, that historic gathering of worldwide bishops in Rome from 1962 through 1965, which altered the course of modern Catholic history. When the *NCR* editors reflected on the Vietnam War, they were writing at a time the council document, "The Pastoral Constitution on the Church in the Modern World," was still in its infancy. That episcopal document called on humanity to form "an entirely new attitude" on war. The world's bishops wrote, in December 1965, that people "must realize that they will have to give a somber reckoning for their deeds of war." Not coincidentally, the words—somber reckonings—made their way into a front-page headline *NCR* published at the conclusion of the Gulf War.

When Hoyt and his colleagues reflected on the Vietnam war, Pope Paul VI had only recently addressed the General Assembly of the United Nations. It was October 4, 1965, when he pleaded with the heads of the world's governments: "No more war; war never again." And when Hoyt and his colleagues reflected on Vietnam, they had none of the insights available to me as editor that had come from three years of U.S. Catholic soul-searching and led to "The Challenge of Peace: God's Promise and Our Response," the U.S. bishops' 1983 pastoral on peace. The process had forced many Catholics (admittedly, by no means the majority) and many other Americans to the conclusion that war and war preparations must be assessed in moral, and not simply strategic terms. The two most significant distinctions in the U.S. public debate over the pending possible war with Iraq relative to earlier U.S. "war" discussions were: (1) the manner in which religious leaders in a majority opposed, and opposed earlier, an armed U.S. response to Saddam Hussein; (2) and the way in which the "moral" debate over the possible war did in fact emerge. To see, before the year ended, U.S. newspapers suddenly engaged in discussion of just-war theory, to hear U.S. politicians reacting to public statements by clerics and cardinals, theologians and moral theorists, was a new element in U.S. political life. What we now know is that it did not alter the outcome.

Still, it did reveal the extent to which Catholic social teaching had inserted itself into the U.S. social debate. Since the Second Vatican Council, and in a multitude of ways, the Catholic Church has proclaimed a continuous, loud and explicit rejection of war.

This statement has been more forceful than at any other time in modern history and probably any other time since the early years of the church. Why? Because it grows out of a collective Catholic revulsion of modern weapons of war and, certainly in part, out of a quarter century of reexamination and renewed appreciation of the Gospels. Modern weapons, the 1965 "Pastoral Constitution on the Church in the Modern World" told us, have brought humanity to "a moment of supreme crisis in its advance toward maturity." Ensuring that the point would not be lost, the U.S. bishops opened the peace pastoral by repeating those very words.

With much of this in mind, I sat down during the second week of August 1990, about 150 days before the first U.S. bombs fell on Iraq, to write an editorial I knew I would have to live with for years. These words appeared in the front-page editorial of our August 24 issue: "In a world of dwindling petroleum supplies, U.S. policy assures that we will remain for years on a warpath. And if the commodity is not oil, then it will be some other considered vital to U.S. interests. . . . Once again, it is the deepening gap between rich and poor today that is the greatest threat to world peace."

The editorial pressed a question that, I felt, begged to be answered. "Why Iraq?" Why the overwhelming U.S. military response in the face of this act of Middle East aggression when other similar acts had been greeted by virtual U.S. silence? Why the outrage this time? There had been none when Turkey invaded Cyprus in 1974 or when Syria gobbled up Lebanon in 1976. Why did the United States press for the implementation of U.N. sanctions against Iraq while being passive—if not hostile—to the implementation of sanctions against Israel in the wake of its continued occupation of the West Bank or Gaza Strip since 1967? To the contrary, instead of speaking out against these aggressors, the Bush administration, we saw, was courting Syria, cajoling Turkey and quietly working with Israel to form the appearances of a strong Middle East coalition.

Bush himself helped to provide the answer. He said that the U.S. military buildup in the Middle East was needed to "protect the American way of life." But by this he was not speaking of the Bill of Rights. Not while he was courting Syrian President Hafez al-Assad, the Middle East's most notorious rights violator.

No, Bush was talking about U.S. opulence. Once again, a U.S. administration was placing economic interests before human interests. Our editorial said, "In the Middle East, as long as oil interests come before Arab interests, there can be no lasting peace. In any event, there eventually will be no oil."

This, of course, was not the first time we had editorialized about the Bush administration's lack of concern for human rights. How often before we had reported and editorialized on its and the Reagan administration's winks in the face of other governments' human rights abuses—if those governments were serving U.S. economic or geopolitical interests. El Salvador has been the most glaring example. I came to *NCR* just three months after the assassination of Archbishop Oscar Romero and just six months before the killings of four U.S. churchwomen in a rural area outside the Salvadoran capital.

Nearly a decade later, in November 1989, Salvadoran militiamen, armed with weapons paid for by U.S. taxpayers, brutally murdered six Jesuits, their housekeeper and her teenage daughter. The U.S. government has never adequately pressed for justice for these crimes. It has turned a blind eye on the 70,000 dead in El Salvador during the 1980s, most carried out by Salvadoran government-sponsored death squads.

Translated from Spanish, *El Salvador* means the Savior. This very Christian nation, victimized so outrageously by the Reagan and Bush administrations, bound Christians in North America to Christians of Latin America as no other nation has during my editorship—though we have made a marked effort in the case of Haiti.

Romero, the four women, the Salvadoran Jesuits and the two women who died with them served as bridges of spirit and understanding and opened the eyes of many North Americans, Christians and others, enabling them to see into the Third World and to look back out again at themselves in a manner most other Americans simply cannot.

This fresh, nonnationalistic perspective explains why so many U.S. Christians did not buy into Bush's war against Iraq. They saw only too clearly the double standard involved. "Human-rights principles must find their way into U.S. financial and economic decision-making," the August 24 editorial said. "Tough stuff, but we will either do it while we can or the future will force us to."

NCR has its share of weaknesses, but supranationalism is not one of them. I have already alluded to our modest but well-focused attempts to introduce readers to the complexities in the Middle East. The paper has excelled in a number of areas of international coverage: Central and South America, particularly. From the mid-1970s onward, writers such as Penny Lernoux and June Carolyn Erlick opened up Latin America—its plight, its people, its politics, its economic oppression, its struggling church, its martyrs—to the North American church.

Erlick was alongside Romero nearly constantly in 1978 and 1979, tracing his steps, profiling him, explaining *why* he was doing and saying what he was doing—and explaining to the readers why he was on the paper's front page. That was Oscar Romero before he became "Oscar Romero—martyr."

During the 1980s, my colleagues and I began to develop the same intensity of coverage on another important dimension of military morality: the deadly trade in weapons. This focus was perhaps best summarized in the early days of Iraq's invasion of Kuwait, in the August 24, 1991, editorial. The subject was U.S. military armaments and the billions being spent on weapons and weapon delivery systems through the Reagan years—billions being spent while pressing domestic needs went unattended. The U.S. government sold weapons to virtually anyone who asked—and had the money to pay. The oil-rich Middle East had the money. Billions of dollars of weapons or weapon-related technology would go one month to Egypt, the next month to Israel, the following month to Turkey, Saudi Arabia, Kuwait or Iraq. We fed Middle East arms stockpiles as if there were no tomorrow. We then feigned great surprise when war broke out. It is neither logical nor moral to play such a major role in arming a region of the world and then to wash our hands of responsibility once the shooting begins.

In the 24 months before Iraq's invasion of Kuwait, there had been a new zest to the peace dove's flight. The additional energy came from an eruption of hope in the months that followed the fall of the Berlin Wall in November 1989. The hope was that U.S. military spending might get serious cutbacks. There was talk of a "peace dividend." The nation's advocates for the poor, for the inner-city minorities, for education and health programs, finally had some reason to believe things could get better, that Cold War money could now be redirected to long-neglected social programs.

But Saddam Hussein's threat conveniently erupted almost as if it were choreographed by Pentagon planners. I must admit I wondered while I wrote that first Gulf War editorial and was still wondering after the Iraqi army was on its knees. This is the reason I inserted the following paragraph into the August 24 editorial: "Meanwhile, those back home who brought us Vietnam and MIRVed our nuclear warheads, and who have been eagerly building Trident submarines and Stealth Bombers, could not be more pleased. It makes one wonder."

But probably the most important overall concept in that editorial was a call to see unfolding events in the context of the growing gap between the rich and poor nations of the world, between the North and the South. "The world's increasingly hungry, oppressed and restless live at desperation's edge. Many nations have become tinderboxes for violence and war."

Catholics, I thought, should make the effort to see the world, and what was happening in the Middle East, through the eyes of their universal church and not through the cyclopean eye of U.S. society—which holds the telescope the wrong way around in order to reduce the size of the problems it surveys. In other words, for "U.S. Catholics," the war was to pull our "U.S." from our "Catholic." In the months of the Iraq buildup and war, *NCR* tried to stress what it means to be truly "Catholic" under such circumstances. With national war fever rising, it was to be no easy task.

This, then, in part, is what we said in the *NCR* August 24 editorial:

> With the Cold War's end, the world's nations have entered a new era requiring farsighted foreign policies, but the growing Iraqi crisis has revealed that the United States remains mired.

> We have all been so preoccupied with the East-West conflict and the need to avert nuclear war between the superpowers that we have given inadequate attention to the growing gap between the world's rich and poor and the domestic and cross-border pressures that have resulted. The gap in per capita income between the developed and developing nations is today twice as large as it was 30 years ago; the gap in public-health expenditures is four times as large.

> With the East-West prism removed, North-South divisions of unprecedented proportions loom. The world's increasingly hungry, oppressed and restless live at desperation's edge. Many nations have become tinderboxes for violence and war.

> When Iraq invaded Kuwait, our Middle East allegiances and foes changed overnight like shifting desert sands. We are reminded of the adage: Nations have no lasting friends, only lasting interests. However, U.S. interests have set us on a course to war in the Middle East.

> Our leaders speak of lofty principles, but our actions are dictated by more selfish policies. One reads: We must assure the free flow of cheap petroleum from the Middle East. We will use military force, if necessary. If this policy were ever questioned, the question was settled two weeks ago when U.S. ground troops were ordered to Saudi Arabia.

In a world of dwindling petroleum supplies, U.S. policy assures that we will remain for years on a warpath. And if the commodity is not oil, it will be some other considered vital to U.S. interests. And if the battle will not be with Arabs, it will be with some other Third World peoples.

The United States constitutes 5 percent of the world's population while it consumes one-third of its resources. To maintain this posture—and increasingly it will require military force—is neither wise nor economically or morally tenable.

U.S. foreign and economic policies—because they are linked—need the kind of public evaluation that this country has never seen. Americans must be shown how their economic life works and who pays the price for it. This public debate must aim at distinguishing apparent from real U.S. interests. These real interests we define as those that preserve world peace and help build a more just world order.

How do we begin?

A public declaration of an evenhanded foreign policy supporting the human-rights principles in our nation's founding documents and the U.N. charter. The implementation of such a policy would help realign the United States with the aspirations of the world's poor and voiceless. But public policy is not enough.

Human-rights principles must find their way into U.S. financial and economic decision-making. Tough stuff, but we either do it while we can or the future will force us to. It is the recognition of the long-term self-interest involved here that offers any hope such an outlook could be adopted.

Once again, it is the deepening gap between rich and poor today that is the greatest threat to world peace. And if we think our peace is not threatened by that global gap, then we also fail to read the significance of the growing gap at home. Our poor have become Third World poor.

Seen in this light, U.S. nationalism must become internationalism, true globalism. The human community must be seen as part of an intricate fabric of life in harmony with the resources that support the planet's life. We must apply the knowledge we have so recently acquired in this half-century, the understanding that humans live not so much within nations as within regions and as part of a single socio-political-economic ecosystem: planet Earth.

In the Middle East, as long as oil interests come before Arab interests, there can be no lasting peace. In any event, there eventually will be no oil. . . .

President Bush spoke of standing up against unjust aggression, but his words have fallen on hot sand. Looking around, the United States finds itself allied in the desert with Turkey, which invaded Cyprus in 1974 and occupies two-thirds of that nation today. It is courting Syria, which intervened in Lebanon in 1976 and maintains forces through 60 percent of Lebanese territory today. (Syria, one needs to recall, has been the U.S.-hostage ringleader and the nation that engineered the 1983 attack on U.S. Marine barracks in Beirut, killing 241 U.S. servicemen.) Moreover, the United States stands ready with Israel, which has occupied the West Bank and Gaza Strip since 1967 and maintains a small enclave in southern Lebanon, all in violation of several U.N. resolutions.

Selective sanctions and double standards do not enhance the use of international law. They do not add to U.S. credibility.

To much of the Arab world, 10 million rich and 140 million poor, the United States has allied itself with feudal families who head oil companies. The poison-gas-wielding Saddam Hussein, meanwhile, widely feared, maintains a popularity in the Arab world that defies the U.S. imagination. He has captured the image of an Arab leader standing up for powerless against the West and their monarchial Arab friends. . . .

As a nation, we are moving with frightening speed—and all too unreflectively—into sinking sand. Or worse, into an all-out Middle East war. . . .

In the desert, Iraq's troops were digging in on Kuwait's border, U.S. and "coalition" troops (this war's word for "allies") were moving into position in Saudi Arabia. At home, the election season was picking up. As Americans prepared to go to the polls in the biennial congressional elections, it appeared that the Middle East situation was perhaps even stabilizing somewhat. The United Nations had voted economic sanctions, and we watched and waited to see them take effect. Despite the troubling aspects of seeing U.S. combat troops introduced into the Middle East and the way the Bush administration was drumming its unilateral military crusade against Saddam Hussein, September and October had provided a kind of "do-we-dare-hope?" interval. Economic sanctions were in place, the most far-reaching ever inflicted upon a nation in modern times, and there was just the hope that in the post-Cold War era the family of nations had found an alternative to war. Indeed, it was evident that far less encompassing sanctions had significantly moved South Africa's government toward ending apartheid.

With such overwhelming evidence for the effectiveness of sanctions, had the world really turned a corner in the fall of 1990? Was it possible that a less belligerent Soviet Union had produced a less belligerent United States? Was it possible that by working through the United Nations we were entering a less militaristic world? I admit to having harbored such hopes.

Such was the mix of moods and reflections as NCR watched the congressional races and the November elections. How could we have known, as the nation voted November 6, that two days later, Desert Shield was to become Desert Storm, that Bush was preparing to announce a doubling of U.S. forces in the Persian Gulf? Many analysts subsequently wrote that it was that fateful decision—to introduce 500,000 troops in the Middle East—that made war almost inevitable. By December, Bush appeared determined to take on Saddam Hussein and it was becoming, it seemed, a war of two personalities. Bush had called up the reserves. He was stepping up pressure—and rhetoric. In public speeches he began to ridicule Saddam Hussein, purposely mispronouncing his name. There would be no room—absolutely none—for compromise or negotiations, Bush insisted, seemingly backing himself into a corner. Saddam Hussein returned the volley. This was a "holy war," he said, against the infidels. This cast Bush as the personification of all evil. The conflict had become so personal it appeared to us, as well as to many others, to be as much a battle of two men's egos as anything else. And it was getting more dangerous with each passing day.

In the newsroom, we decided the time had come to do something special in order to share with our readers our growing fears. We wanted to do something visually striking as well as editorially solid for the December 14 issue. One suggestion was for a front page filled with the words: THE WAR OF THE EGOS. I countered with the idea of a front page containing the words from Pope Paul VI's October 1965 U.N. address: NO MORE WAR; WAR NEVER AGAIN! We assembled an issue that contained a number of views on the looming war, including a sampling of street opinions from across America. However, it was now only one day before press time and there was a general feeling in the newsroom that Pope Paul VI's words were not working. The spacing was not right and the eye-catching, dramatic effect we had hoped to achieve just wasn't there. At this point, senior editor Michael Farrell volunteered to put together a collage of graphic photographs from other wars. Superimposed on Artist Farrell's dramatic collage were the words NO MORE WAR. (See illustration page 36.)

The collage referred readers to a back-page editorial that quoted from Pope Paul's October 1965 U.N. address and rested under an

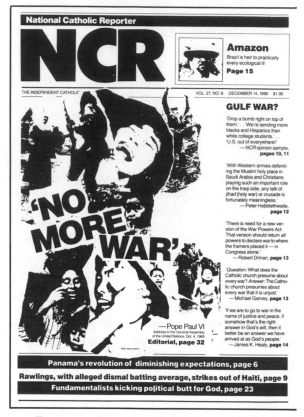

National Catholic Reporter

NCR

Amazon
Brazil is heir to practically every ecological ill
Page 15

THE INDEPENDENT CATHOLIC*   VOL. 27, NO. 8   DECEMBER 14, 1990 $1.00

'NO MORE WAR'

—Pope Paul VI
Address to the General Assembly of the United Nations, Oct. 4, 1965
Editorial, page 32

GULF WAR?

'Drop a bomb right on top of them.'... 'We're sending more blacks and Hispanics than white college students.'... 'U.S. out of everywhere!'
—NCR opinion sample, **pages 10, 11**

'With Western armies defending the Muslim holy place in Saudi Arabia and Christians playing such an important role on the Iraqi side, any talk of jihad (holy war) or crusade is fortunately meaningless.'
—Peter Hebblethwaite, **page 12**

'There is need for a new version of the War Powers Act. That version should return all powers to declare war to where the framers placed it — in Congress alone.'
—Robert Drinan, **page 13**

'Question: What does the Catholic church presume about every war? Answer: The Catholic church presumes about every war that it is unjust.'
—Michael Garvey, **page 13**

'If we are to go to war in the name of justice and peace, if somehow that's the right answer in God's will, then it better be an answer we have arrived at as God's people.'
—James K. Healy, **page 14**

Panama's revolution of diminishing expectations, page 6

Rawlings, with alleged dismal batting average, strikes out of Haiti, page 9

Fundamentalists kicking political butt for God, page 23

Front page from Dec. 14, 1990 issue of *NCR*.

editorial headline: "We must speak out, we must take to the streets."

The editorial argued that going to war over oil was immoral and could, in addition, cause as many as 45,000 U.S. and 100,000 Iraqi deaths. (It turned out to be fortunately wrong on its U.S. count but tragically prescient on the latter figure.) We called for a nationwide mobilization against the war, stating that it would have to consist of relatives, spouses and friends of soldiers in the Gulf along with religious, antiwar and pacifist groups. "It will take millions of people and a constant bleating of the pipes of peace to penetrate this administration's ignorance and arrogance," the editorial stated. It concluded that to go to war would be immoral.

In retrospect, the editorial contained much wishful thinking. Large numbers of protesters never took to the streets, not until it was too late, not until the U.S. Air Force and Navy had begun to strike at Iraq. Further, we underestimated the virtual dictatorial power of a modern president when it comes to deciding to go to war. If any way did exist to halt Bush's seeming urge to fight in the Gulf, it had to be through Congress. Congress, however, had accumulated a dismal record on harnessing presidential powers since Vietnam, despite the fact that the Constitution explicitly states that "Congress shall have the power . . . to declare war."

Who could stop Bush? What about the War Powers Act? One person who understood well the legalities involved in the struggle to limit presidential war powers was *NCR* columnist Jesuit Father Robert Drinan. I first met Drinan in Vietnam in 1969 when he came over as part of a fact-finding team which I was to guide. The former five-term Massachusetts congressman had been writing for *NCR* since he opted against reelection, leaving Congress in 1980 after Pope John Paul II said he did not want priests in government or politics. The newsroom joke, of course, was that the edict applied everywhere except in Poland, where priests—and a pope— were always politically influential in determining who ran the government and how and when they did it. As a congressman, Drinan could always be counted on as an advocate for the poor. He accomplished many legislative feats but will go down in history for having been a member of the House Judiciary Committee that voted three articles of impeachment against President Richard Nixon, July 30, 1974. That sealed Nixon's fate; only five weeks later, at midday on August 9, 1974, Nixon resigned. Just after Drinan left his congressional seat, I contacted him and offered him a regular writing spot on *NCR*'s pages. A decade later, faced with the need to address the topic of how to stop Bush, I called Drinan and asked him to write a column explaining what was at stake, and what was possible.

One of the Constitutional questions the nation faced as it approached a possible war against Iraq was whether Bush had the authority unilaterally to commit the nation to war. During Vietnam, Congress began deliberations on the War Powers Resolution in an effort to strike a compromise between what the Constitution states and the conceivable need of a president to enter war in a national emergency. During his time in Congress, Drinan had been involved in the War Powers Resolution vote. As we discussed what would best serve the readers, we talked about those early 1970s deliberations. Drinan decided he would write a column outlining Congress' intent at the time, and he would review the lasting effects of the legislation. What he had to say related directly to what many saw as a potentially serious constitutional crisis. The following is taken from Drinan's column in the December 14 issue:

Although the Constitution seems clear and categorical when it states that "Congress shall have power . . . to declare war," American presidents have engaged in military hostilities on more than 150 occasions without a declaration of war by Congress. Indeed, the congressional declarations of war before World War I and World War II seemed to be the exceptions.

As the Vietnam War was ending, Congress sought to rectify this situation. It recognized that, in a dangerous world where at least seven nations have nuclear weapons, the president needs a bit more flexibility than the Constitution apparently gives him.

As a result, Congress in the War Powers Resolution in 1973 conceded the necessity of allowing the president to introduce the U.S. armed forces "into situations where imminent involvement in hostilities is clearly indicated by the circumstances." But the president "in every possible instance shall consult with Congress" before he acts.

In addition, the president must submit to Congress within 48 hours of his action a report setting forth the circumstances that made his action necessary. If Congress fails to act within 60 days, the president shall terminate any use of U.S. armed forces. That 60-day period may be extended for no more than an additional 30 days if the president certifies that an additional delay of a month is necessary for the safety of U.S. armed personnel.

As a member of Congress, I had a great deal of difficulty with the concessions offered to the president in the War Powers Act. I voted against the measure in the House and voted no, again, on the conference report. When President Nixon vetoed the measure, I, along with several others, voted to override the veto on the theory that the War Powers Act, however limited, was better than having no control at all over the president's unilateral action leading to war.

To the astonishment of everyone, President Nixon's veto was overridden and the War Powers Act became the law of the land Nov. 7, 1973. Congress and the country could at least say there would be no more Vietnams.

But, alas, no president has agreed to abide by the War Powers Act. Military attacks in Libya, Grenada and Panama have been carried out with no use of the War Powers Act—except perhaps some consultations with the leaders of Congress. . . .

Again, Congress alone by the Constitution has the power to "raise and support armies . . . to provide and maintain a navy . . . and to make rules for the . . . regulation of the land and naval forces." To be sure, the president, under the Constitution, "shall be commander-in-chief to initiate a war. The president is authorized to engage in armed hostilities only according to the terms of the War Powers Act.

It is unlikely the Congress will be aggressive in seeking to exercise its exclusive right to declare war. If the war is undertaken and goes badly, the Congress can blame the president. If the war goes well, the Congress can rejoice in the new unity and solidarity of the United Nations, which authorized the war.

The Congress enacted the best possible compromise available on the issue of war in 1973. Since that time, the menace of communism has faded away. As a result, the alleged need for the president to be able to launch an invasion without congressional authorization has diminished.

Consequently, there is need for a new version of the War Powers Act. That version should return *all* power to declare war to where the framers placed it—in Congress alone.

Facing the prospects of a major war, many American communities, including church groups, did much soul-searching. Many were developing opinions, and many of those opinions changed from week to week. For the December 14 issue, *NCR* reporters and stringers around the nation interviewed Americans wherever they found them, to sample their views. It was not meant to be a scientific sampling. When we embarked on the project, which involved at least a score of reporters, I had hoped we would find more opposition to the war than we did. What we found was a mixture of sentiments and personal confusion. We filled a page with these comments, starting with one somewhat tangled opinion not uncharacteristic of others. Patricia Jones of Council Bluffs, Iowa, answered *NCR's* question, "If you were President Bush, what would you do?" by saying, "Drop a bomb right on top of them (Iraqis). That would keep anyone else from trying to pull this. . . . But sometimes I wonder why we're doing this. We have a way of sticking our nose where it doesn't belong." Conclusion: troubled, yes; pacifist, no; ready for action, yes. In the same issue, *NCR* columnist Michael O. Garvey, who likes to claim that good religious education ended with the abandonment of the traditional Catholic catechism, wrote a short article containing two sentences that I wish would appear on the back of every Catholic's hand in America. In the style of his favorite catechism, Garvey wrote: "*Q*: What does the Catholic church presume about every war? *A*: The Catholic church presumes about every war that it is unjust."

Garvey comes out of the Catholic Worker movement, a Catholic pacifist movement. It is said that his family celebrates the birthdays of movement founders, Dorothy Day and Peter Maurin, every year. The Catholic Worker movement, which teaches Christian pacifism, agrarianism and socialism, has had an enduring influence on U.S. Catholics since its beginnings in the New York Bowery. There, more than 60 years ago, Day and Maurin opened the first Catholic Worker house of hospitality.

The Worker movement has since provided a good share of the moral underpinnings for Catholic opposition to war. Just one ready example of the Worker's influence on people who then further influenced antiwar writing and pro-peace activities: Jesuit Father Dan Berrigan and his brother, Phil, both faithful pacifists, have traced some of their thinking on war to Dorothy Day and the Catholic Workers. Although I was not myself a young Catholic Worker, I was a young Berrigan admirer, and we named our son, Daniel, after him in 1973.

Our family's Worker involvement began with the move to Kansas City and *NCR*. For many years, we attended weekly Mass at the Shalom Catholic Worker House in Kansas City, Kansas. The influence of Father Dick Wempe and Benedictine Sister Barbara McCracken was direct. Readers familiar with *NCR* will know that the peace-teaching supplements that have appeared periodically through the 1980s were written and prepared by McCracken. Although Wempe is now retired—and Shalom house continues to provide hospitality to the homeless, often Guatemalans or Salvadoran refugees, or Mexicans looking for modest jobs to support their families back home—his program of speakers during the 1980s provided important encouragement to my work at *NCR*.

In the chapters ahead, we look at the war. We look at war-making and vanquished peacemaking. Through the unfolding half-dozen issues of *NCR*, we look at war as we tried to find our role as Christians and commentators (and as activists, too, though the individual participation of some staff members in peace protests in Kansas City and Washington, D.C., were as private persons, not as journalists). The hope is that, as our war coverage for peacemakers unfolds in these pages, we can all find lessons that will better prepare us for when the United States takes off on its next military adventure.

3

Lonely Sorrow

We prepared for the worst. We prepared for war. As the world stopped turning and approached the January 15, U.N.-imposed deadline—which allegedly legitimized the use of force against Saddam Hussein's forces in the Persian Gulf—we in the *NCR* newsroom scrambled to assemble two possible versions of the weekly paper that would be dated January 25, 1991: one in the event of war, the other if the war was still on hold. (From a strictly detached, editorial point of view, if war were to begin, I wanted it early in the week to allow us time to gather reactions and sort out events. Monday or Tuesday would be ideal; Wednesday, okay; Thursday or Friday, the day we go to press, difficult to impossible. Admittedly, editors look at life with an eye to publishing deadlines.) The bombing began around 6:00 p.m. Wednesday, January 16, dinnertime in the heartland.

Throughout the war, I felt that my job called me to be at least two people, the detached editor and the engaged Catholic pacifist. In some ways, those two people seemed to compete against each other; in others, they complemented each other. It is said there are only two kinds of editors, one who can edit any publication, another who edits to put out a paper he or she wants to read. As *NCR* editor, I have always seen myself in the latter camp. That said, I also believe the way to put out the brightest publication is to allow the staff wide latitude to follow its best journalistic judgments and instincts. As a result, *NCR* ends up each week the product of collective energies that I attempt to harness and direct. At least that's the theory.

Covering the war was a special challenge. We wanted to give our readers information and opinion not generally found in other publications. The content, space and placement of an *NCR* article is generally determined by several questions. Does it provide information not found elsewhere? Does it read well? Will it hold a reader's interest? Throughout the war, I used my column, "Inside NCR," to share my personal feelings. I knew how distressed I was, how alone I felt in my sorrow, how lonely the war had become. I assumed most *NCR* readers felt much as I did, and I presumed that by sharing my feelings I could perhaps help them, too, to break through their sense of isolation and sadness. I was sad and angry.

My feelings stemmed from knowing this was an unnecessary war. I felt that sanctions had not been given their proper chance and would have worked had they been given the chance. Although they were commonly regarded as the most effective in recorded history, with the potential of cutting Iraq's gross national product by 50 percent in the first year, Bush would not wait. In fact, he ignored the evidence. One study stated that sanctions causing a 3 percent decline were already considered successful. Iraq was on its way to a 50 percent decline in a matter of months. I had wanted to see sanctions work; I believed that sanctions could become a key part in nonviolent conflict resolution on a global scale. That week in my column (Jan. 25), my bitterness showed:

> It became a celebration of U.S. technology, a living arms bazaar. Star Wars, laser-guided bombs down ventilation holes in Iraqi command buildings. Most impressive. The gleeful message: Buy U.S. or die.

> There will be hell to pay.

> Also for sale: the notion this will be a *clean* war. It is laudable that at the outset U.S. policymakers feel compelled to limit civilian casualties. Wars, however, are never clean.

That first week of the war was painful. For me, that week and the final week of bombing were the worst of the war. The first week reopened war wounds I had thought long healed. It was bad for my wife, Hoa, as well. We comforted each other but probably played into each other's hurts as well. I told Hoa that first evening of the war that I would start a fast. I stopped eating solid foods, limiting myself to vegetable and fruit drinks, to soups and an occasional liquid diet supplement. I never knew why I was fasting or how long I would fast. It was difficult to explain to others because I did not fully know myself. Hoa never asked about it. She seemed to understand. After the first two days, the hunger left, but I craved foods. The fast kept me grounded in the reality of other people's hardships, and that was good. In any case, I had lost 12 pounds before I quit two weeks later.

The war captured the attention of the nation in personal ways, *NCR* staff included. Throughout the war, the staff seemed especially sensitive to one another's needs. One morning, a staff member spoke about her sense of loneliness and isolation from family and relatives who supported the war. Layout editor Chris Curry actually got sick, his resistance seemingly worn down by events. He was unable to shake the flu for several weeks. Those were stressful days.

Each morning, we began by talking about what we had seen on television the night before or had read in the morning paper. We shared reactions and feelings. This was good therapy, but it also led to a pooling of information out of which came story ideas for coming issues. We began to take more late-breaking stories; we pushed back deadlines. Our ambitions competed with the unforgiving Friday press deadline.

January 16, 1991, will be recorded as that day in history when the United States went to war in the Middle East. It should also be remembered as the day U.S. church leaders parted ways from the U.S. government on matters of war and peace. As early as November, several prominent Catholic leaders had publicly stepped into the debate on the side of peace. Los Angeles Archbishop Roger

Mahony, as president of the bishops' international policy committee, had written a letter to Secretary of State James Baker, dated
November 7, outlining traditional Catholic just-war teaching as it
applied to the situation in the Gulf. Mahony suggested that a war
against Iraq at that time could not be considered moral. When the
nation's 300 Catholic bishops gathered in Washington, D.C., November 12-14 for their annual meeting, Iraq became the major item
on their early agenda, partly because of Mahony's letter. The discussion resulted in the president of the U.S. bishops' conference,
Cincinnati Archbishop Daniel Pilarczyk, writing a letter to President Bush warning that a U.S military action "could well violate"
Catholic moral teaching.

NCR's front-page headline that week (Nov. 23 issue) read:
"Bishops' president warns Bush of Gulf concerns." And one of
those bishops who had gathered in Washington would provide
perhaps the most poignant people-to-people story of the encroach-
ing war-talk. Detroit Auxiliary Bishop Thomas Gumbleton had
gone to Iraq as part of a delegation seeking the release of the U.S.
hostages held by Saddam Hussein for more than three months.
While he was there, he had met with a Christian family in
Baghdad (there are more than half a million Christians in Iraq's
capital). Gumbleton talked with the parents of three teenagers, parents who knew—as Gumbleton also knew—that if war broke out,
their home, their sons, their lives might all be forfeited.

It should be noted, then, that Bush committed U.S. soldiers to
battle without the blessing of the nation's religious leaders. That
was a first. The overwhelming U.S. religious leadership consensus
on the eve of the U.S. bombings was one of strong opposition to
U.S. military action.

The commencement of the war against Iraq, it is more clear
looking back, gave U.S. Christians a unique opportunity to take
measure of their commitments to nonviolent alternatives to war.
The war became a looking glass through which U.S. Christians, as
church, could catch images of themselves with a unique clarity.
The bad news was the patently unreflective willingness on the part

of the American populace to succumb to the drumbeats of war coming out of the White House and Pentagon. The good news was that most U.S. religious leaders did not fall into that trap. At least this, it appears, bodes well for the future.

If our church leaders are committed to peace paths today, as they weren't only a decade ago, then our children will grow up with more peace-affirming values, and the nation could well develop a different character in the generation to come. Ironically, at the moment of U.S. peacemakers' greatest failure, one can find seeds of future success. We did not expect to find—but were pleased that we did—a virtually unanimous objection by mainline religious leaders to the war Bush was selling to the nation. We published a sampling of Christian leadership views on the war in our January 25 issue. A sampling of those views follows:

> For what reason has our nation unleashed the greatest military force since the Vietnam War? Are we not justified in suspecting that the reason is primarily economic, having to do with unimpeded access to oil? Have we not sent our young men and women to the Persian Gulf, as our president has said, "to protect the American way of life"? But what way of life is it that allows the homeless and unemployed to huddle on our streets and our inner cities to decay? Is it possible that the American "way of life"—unbridled consumption—has not become for many millions a "way of death," unendurable poverty?
>
> — Presiding Bishop Edmond Browning
> American Episcopal Church
>
> . . . We call upon President Bush, as a manifestation of his faith in God as revealed in Jesus Christ, to pursue every possible political and diplomatic avenue—however lengthy—as a primary option.
>
> — President Bishop Leroy Hodapp,
> United Methodist Church

I believe . . . that unless you bend every effort to avoid war, including allowing much more time for sanctions to take effect, you will be responsible for leading the United States and the world into one of the darkest chapters of human history.

> — Bishop Herbert Chilstrom
> Evangelical·Lutheran Church
> of America

The steady drumbeat of war messages from you and your administration have sent a shocking message and we are very concerned. We want you, in turn, to hear the clear message from the religious community: Do not lead the U.S. into war with Iraq.

> — Reverend Paul Sherry,
> President, United Church of Christ

I fear that talk of "minimal" casualties underestimates the uncertainties of war and the grief of a parent—American or Iraqi—who loses a child to war. . . . We fear that war in this situation will destroy many lives, divide our nation and leave the world in a condition which none of us can predict.

> — Archbishop Daniel Pilarczyk,
> President, National Conference
> of Catholic Bishops.

Just a few hours before Bush began the bombing, his own bishop, Episcopal Bishop Edmond Browning, came to the White House in an effort to dissuade him from taking military action. Browning spoke to Bush and reportedly left the meeting sad and shaken by the president's obstinacy.

Among those objecting loudest to the looming war was Pope John Paul II. The pope sent eleventh-hour messages to both President Bush and Saddam Hussein. The following is an excerpt from an article *NCR* Vatican affairs writer Peter Hebblethwaite filed just hours before the bombings began:

"Yes, peace is still possible," said Pope John Paul II Jan. 12 in his annual address to diplomats, "and war would be a setback for the whole of humanity."

John Paul was obstinate in his conviction that peace was possible even as the deadline approached and was passed. Midnight Jan. 15 was 6 a.m. Roman time. The pope was preparing for Mass in his private chapel.

Eleventh-hour messages to President George Bush and Saddam Hussein had been handed to their ambassadors to the Holy See, Thomas Melady and Wissam Chawkat al-Zahawi, Jan. 14.

The pope urged Bush to "avoid a devastating and tragic war." He wrote, "The suffering and destruction of war could only give rise to further injustices. The use of such weapons can never bring adequate solutions to such international problems." He exhorted Bush to "a last-minute effort at dialogue to restore sovereignty to Kuwait and to reestablish international order throughout the Middle East.

The message to Saddam Hussein was tailored slightly differently. He was warned of "the tragic consequences" that war would bring for thousands of people in the Gulf region.

The pope appealed to Saddam Hussein, for the second time in the week, to "make a generous gesture toward peace in the region."

About the same time the pope was pleading with Bush and Saddam to avoid another Middle East tragedy, debate had finally begun in the U.S. Congress. For months after the administration had successfully argued that any sign of division would play into Saddam's hands, the Congress had been silent on the Persian Gulf buildup. Only in the final hours before the January 15 U.N. deadline was the muzzle lifted. I watched many of the speeches live on television and rebroadcast late into the night. After a while they began to blur, as many arguments—pro and con—were repeated from the floor of Congress.

One speech stood out. More than any of the others, it addressed the potential cost of the war in lost lives. That address was delivered by Oregon's Republican Senator, Mark Hatfield, a pacifist. We printed his speech in our January 25 issue. The following is excerpted from Hatfield's remarks:

We have all heard the president's promise: This will not be "another Vietnam." We also know that that's thinly veiled code for "we'll hit them with everything we've got. Straight away. No hesitation." The obvious implication is that this was will be quick and easy and clean.

Indeed, the Pentagon is now doing everything possible to give us the impression that war will come in a tidy little package. Even the words are neat and tidy—body bags are not body bags anymore. That's too messy. That conjures up the wrong images—images of blood and pain and suffering. Now body bags are "human remains pouches." There, America, doesn't that make you feel better? Your sons and daughters and mothers and fathers will have their faces blown off, their limbs torn apart, their chests ripped open, but they won't come home in body bags. They'll come home in neat and tidy human remains pouches.

Mr. President, war isn't quick and easy and clean. It's horrible. It's agonizing. In the midst of battle, war is often as random as it is violent. Innocent people lose their lives; the children and spouses and the parents of people like you and me lose their lives simply because they happen to be in the wrong place at the wrong time. . . .

Maybe it will all be over in a matter of hours—or a matter of days—or a matter of weeks at the outside.

Even if it is, Mr. President, at what cost? At what cost in human lives? How many lost lives can we accept? 100? 1,000? 10,000? And who decides?

Also in *NCR* that week was a piece written by *NCR* and *Washington Post* syndicated columnist Colman McCarthy, who began his writing career with *NCR* in 1966, before he became a speech writer for Sargent Shriver, who was then head of the office of Economic Opportunity in the Johnson administration. When he is not writing, McCarthy, a pacifist, teaches nonviolent conflict resolution in Washington area schools. He founded an organization, Center for Teaching Peace, dedicated to getting courses on nonviolence into U.S. schools. *NCR* has highlighted his work. Wrote McCarthy in our January 25 issue, looking back to Iraq's invasion of Kuwait and the U.S. government's reaction to it: "The five-month war of threats between Bush and Saddam was a textbook example of how not to manage conflict." He went on to list four classic conflict-management techniques that everyone should attempt to memorize and live by. (1) Identify the root cause, not the surface cause, of the fight. (2) Clarify the difference between what is wanted and what is needed. (3) Avoid overreaction. (4) Remember that negotiation is not capitulation. McCarthy wrote:

> Bush's rejection of the force of economic sanctions against the Iraqi government reveals his contempt for a nonviolent solution. He tells Saddam: Withdraw or you're history. Bush has chosen to dictate to a dictator, saying, in effect, you acted murderously, now we'll be the murderers.
>
> It's language Saddam understands. He may be content to have found an adversary thickheaded enough to speak it. Had Bush been a reasonable man, Saddam would have had problems. He might have been persuaded to be rational himself.

Alas, these speak to lost opportunities. We will never know what might have been if, say, sanctions had been given a chance, or if Bush would have taken one of McCarthy's courses.

In the early morning hours of January 17, the pope was awakened with the news that hostilities had begun. He remarked, "In these hours of great dangers, I would like to repeat forcefully that war cannot be an adequate means for solving problems existing between nations. It never has been and never will." The pope expressed "deep sadness," adding that his "sorrow derives from the thought of the victims and is made more acute by the fact that the beginning of this war also marks a grave defeat for international law and the international community." We, too, were heartbroken. Once again, violence had been the chosen method for settling a dispute. Apparently, nothing that had been said on behalf of non-violence had made a difference.

Throughout this crisis, the thought kept recurring that our churches need to move from words to actions. To do more than lament violence. What if, for example, religious leaders would have forbidden young men and women to participate in a war which they (the leaders) had deemed unjust? After all, the Catholic bishops have forbidden the ending of life in the womb. Why not forbid the ending of life in war as well? There would be consistency. People would understand. I kept thinking to myself that not enough Christians had been willing to take personal risks to show their opposition to the war. Not enough were willing to confront Bush and his administration, even when they believed that what he was preparing to do was immoral.

It was a very depressing time. We were entering a dark moment in U.S. history. In the newsroom we agreed that the country would one day come to regret it. We decided to express our sorrow by outlining a front page editorial with large black lines (January 25 issue).

Front page from Jan. 25, 1991 issue of *NCR*.

We also used that editorial to recommit ourselves for the long haul:

There is almost a mythic coincidence to the fact that the scriptural arguments used in Catholic teaching for peace and against war came from the same sand and deserts and towns where war currently is being waged.

There is an almost historic setback in the fact that as the Catholic church slowly becomes identified as a "peace church," its teaching seems to carry so little weight: The moment the decision was made by President George Bush to bomb Iraq, the peacemakers had lost.

The feelings in much of the peace community began with growing frustration, then metamorphosed into an anger that in turn gave way to profound sorrow and, inevitably, prayer.

Peacemakers on Jan. 16 had reason to feel overwhelmed, defeated, crushed. And it takes courage to recommit ourselves to peace work when the returns are so few. But recommit we must, because we have promises to keep.

We have promised to teach the next generation, by giving birth to that generation. We must answer to our children. It is not enough to tell them that violence begets violence. We have to tell them *why* we believe that way. And, fortunately, we can.

Less than a decade ago, the Catholic bishops of this warmaking superpower addressed themselves to "The Challenge of Peace: God's Promise and Our Response."

Much of the church joined in, and together we built a peace pastoral on the strong blocks of the biblical teaching that are our peacemaking heritage.

The letter explained that "the Catholic tradition on war and peace is a long and complex one, reaching from the Sermon on the Mount to the statements of Pope John Paul II." But that Catholic tradition still is not fully understood, even by all Catholics.

The peace pastoral begins with a quotation from the Second Vatican Council (1962-65) statement on modern warfare: "The whole human race faces a moment of supreme crisis in its advance toward maturity." That crisis is very much with us today.

After an introduction, the pastoral presented Old and New Testament arguments in the development of peace-making. Now is an appropriate time to read, *for the first time in earnest for some of us,* the scriptural—particularly the New Testament—basis for that 1983 pastoral letter.

If within our lives, nation and world violence still reigns, the path of nonviolence is no less correct. Our efforts remain firm, our eyes—and hopes—fixed upon our children and those generations still to come.

This editorial led directly to a series of excerpts taken from the bishops' peace pastoral, "The Challenge of Peace: God's Promise and Our Response," excerpts grounded in the New Testament. One in particular has stayed with me. I thought about it repeatedly during the war. Perhaps it will help explain why *NCR* viewed the Iraq war as it did, or why I felt *NCR* could not have viewed the war any other way:

> In all of his suffering, as in all of his life and ministry, Jesus refused to defend himself with force or with violence. He endured violence and cruelty so that God's love might be fully reconciled to the One from whom it had become estranged. Even at the time of his death, Jesus cried out for forgiveness for those who were his executioners: "Father, forgive them" (Luke 23:24).

The "boards," those pages we put together to be taken to the printer, were finished. We felt exhausted. Not because of the work. Once the paper is completed, there is often a kind of quiet exhilaration stemming from the satisfaction of having finished another issue. No, this exhaustion flowed like a river of sorrow deep within. I knew I felt it within myself. And from the looks in the eyes of the staff, it was within them too. That weekend, at home with the family, I decided that the following week the paper needed a good jolt. We needed to shake the depression. We needed a change of course.

4

Twelve Steps

Monday morning, January 21, I was on the telephone first thing. I wanted to get a broader feel for how people were reacting to the bombing, then in its fifth day. What I had earlier found, from conversations with personal friends and others who had for months been protesting the war, was widespread discouragement. For months, many thousands had worked to avert a U.S. military response. But their efforts had failed. For example, in Kansas City about 200 peace activists had, among other actions, gathered faithfully for an hour each Sunday afternoon to line the streets at a major intersection. They held peace signs, some calling upon motorists to honk their horns for peace. On a few occasions, Hoa and I took our teenage children to these demonstrations and they, too, stood, stomping their cold feet to keep warm as they lined the curbs. One day, they will remember why they stood in the cold, we thought.

There was still hope then, even if it was slim, that somehow these and other demonstrations might wake up enough people who would, in turn, demand that the administration find a peaceful means of resolving the Gulf crisis. And, even if the Kansas City protesters did not succeed, they would say, at least they did *something* to show they did not agree with the course Bush was on. At least they had been visible.

However, now that the bombs were falling, what was to be said and what was to be done? Many peace activists were uncertain about what needed to be done. Many with whom I spoke that day and through the rest of the week seemed to be holding to their present course, chiefly remaining faithful to their protests and maintaining patience in their ways. Yet, what still seemed frequently lacking was the sense of immediate direction: What could be done to resist or oppose the war? Military briefers were already becoming familiar as they recorded the tally of air sorties, running then more than 2,000 daily. They were claiming precision accuracy, but their very insistence seemed to cover a darker truth. As the pope had said a few days before, the outbreak of bombing represented a defeat for the international community. For U.S. peace activists in particular, it was also a personal setback.

These peace activists, after all, were the ones who had worked through the 1980s to curb U.S. militarism. They were the ones who had lobbied over the years to end military aid to Central American human-rights abusers. They were the ones who had lobbied to halt the billions being spent on nuclear weapons systems that, incidentally, a decade later were found to have no strategic purpose. During that first week of bombing—as the Pentagon released videos of "smart bombs" being guided through the front doors of bunkers and down the ventilation pipe of what was said to be an enemy command post—it was being said that President Reagan's Star Wars technology was paying off. But the truth is that "smart bomb" technology and the much acclaimed Patriot missile defense system predated Reagan, whose military legacy was the buildup of forever useless nuclear weapons and delivery systems.

Yes, January was difficult for peace advocates. Peace activists had taken the U.S. bishops' 1983 peace pastoral seriously. They had tried to introduce it into the schools and parishes. They had made that "conscious choice," of which Pope John Paul spoke at Hiroshima in 1981, to reject modern armaments so that "humanity can survive." These peace advocates had hoped that Vietnam had taught the nation lasting lessons about the folly of war. They had hoped that lessons had been learned about the futility of trying to impose, through force, a political solution on a distant Third World nation. They had hoped that lessons had been learned about the long-term and hidden costs in waging war, and about the domestic neglect resulting from it.

Peace advocates had labored for a decade or more almost entirely without recognition and without material reward. Ironically, they had been among those who were seriously making the effort to build that "kinder and gentler nation" to which Bush had given lip service. Was round-the-clock bombing of a Third World nation the work of a "kinder and gentler" nation? Might it just be possible, these peace advocates had dared to wonder before Iraq's invasion of Kuwait, that in the 1990s their nation might rediscover its true greatness? That it might find this greatness in its ideas and idealism? That it might return to this idealism after the decades of the confused 1970s and the greedy 1980s?

No, it was not to be. The bombs falling on Iraq had put an end to those dreams. Worse yet, a sick and unreflective war euphoria was beginning to spread across the nation. With the bombs, we were beginning to be told, had come a reassertion of American will. It all felt very sick.

I heard discouragement in the dozens of conversations I had that week. I kept asking myself what I could do, what the paper could say, what might make a difference. I considered that most people connect at a deeper level when they share feelings as well as ideas. I wanted to connect people, to let them know they were not alone and to tell them that many others were feeling just as they were. The sense of loneliness and isolation we all felt at the time, I knew, was not in the long term either healthy or useful. Unchecked, it could lead to apathy and even despair. Yet, overwhelmingly, what I was picking up in conversations that week were feelings of powerlessness and isolation. I heard people speak of sadness coming from feeling cut off from neighbors, family and friends who supported the war. U.S. flags had been hoisted in shopping malls, on factories and office buildings and in front of homes across America. This was, perhaps, an understandable and even laudable expression of concern and support for young U.S. men and women who had been sent to the Persian Gulf. But to many war opponents, the flags also represented support for a U.S. military policy with which they strongly disagreed. It made flying the flag difficult. One friend in New Jersey, commenting on all the flags on his block, said he wondered when "the neighborhood flag committee" would come knocking to ask him why he had not put out his flag. A Kansas activist told me that he was disappointed he did not have the courage to fly his flag upside down, an internationally understood sign of distress.

Three years ago, President Bush had wrapped himself in the flag at every possible moment in his election efforts. That was hardly new in American politics. I thought it was abusive and said so editorially.

As for myself I had grown up waving flags. I could not hold enough of them during those Fourth of July parades as I walked from my elementary school to the local Milwaukee park. But later in life, especially during the Vietnam years, I saw the flag used as a symbol of support for U.S. militarism overseas. I was appalled to see so many miniature flags painted on jet bombers and fighter planes on U.S. air bases in Vietnam. Love of country frequently requires a detached view, not a lockstep mentality, I have long believed. Since Vietnam, I have had trouble singing the national anthem. I stand at sporting events and turn to the flag, but I do not sing. I see this as a war scar and feel badly about it.

There was an exception a year or so back. I took my wife and children to the Moscow circus when it was in town. At the conclusion of the circus acts, in a grand final display of friendship and peace, with U.S. and Soviet flags being waved together, the entire audience stood to listen to the Soviet national anthem. At its conclusion, "The Star-Spangled Banner" began to play. I found myself, quite unexpectedly, singing it for the first time in years. My children, surprised, looked at me in disbelief. Tears were running down my cheeks. Here was the best of nationalism: friendship, cooperation and mutual admiration. Not arrogant nationalism that leads to war. It had taken a circus to heal wounds I had carried for years.

I think that what makes our nation great is the U.S. Constitution and Bill of Rights, radical documents with provisions all too willingly trampled on by government leaders, especially in wartime. We hold the highest of ideals: "liberty and justice for all." But why, I have wondered, is there always more said about the former than the latter.

What makes America great is our ethnic mix, which challenges us. Were we really to learn to live together in modest harmony, we would set an example for the entire human family. We are also blessed with rich natural resources, although sadly we have abused and spent them as few other nation's ever have. So I embrace our nation, even as I dream that one day nations all go the way of ancient city-states, stepping stones on the historical evolutionary path to a wiser and more fruitful world. I have often asked myself if one day "nationalism" might be listed among the great church heresies. Increasingly, it is becoming viewed as dysfunctional and interfering with regional biosystems, out of step with the ecological and human insights of the late 20th century. The greater challenge—central to my Christian faith—is to embrace all the world's family and to keep my nation from trampling upon others, especially the many weaker and poorer nations of the world. My faith also holds that I must work for justice in order to protect the weak and marginalized of the world. The United States, we know so well, represents only 5 percent of the world's people, but it consumes more than a third of its resources. This knowledge places special responsibilities upon us. It is also key to how we must look at wars, especially when our government leaders talk about fighting them to "protect American interests." This could and often does mean protecting, upholding and increasing current injustices.

Further, blind nationalism is self-defeating. The human family, I firmly believe, can grow and prosper only if we attend to the pressing justice questions that frame reality today. These were some of the important assumptions that I, as *NCR* editor, attempted to bring to our war coverage. I think many who were protesting the war, including U.S. church groups, shared these assumptions. Painfully lacking in the wider media during those weeks when it might have made a difference was any sustained discussion of these thoughts. Many in the peace movement were saying these things, but coverage of the protesters usually only went as far as showing pictures of their signs. This was a disservice to both the protesters and to the rest of the nation.

I felt it important to try to report on the peace movement with more depth. With this in mind, I asked *NCR* staff writer Demetria Martinez to talk to leaders within it and profile the movement itself. It was an effort to bring added light to what these people were saying to the nation. Images of demonstrators had been getting on television, and some of their views were being picked up by the newspapers. However, no publication I had seen had attempted a profile. If they had, those reporters would have learned, as Martinez found, an interesting fact being overlooked. Unlike in the 1960s, these antiwar demonstrations were drawing more U.S minorities, blacks in particular. Bush had made a tactical mistake by either setting or allowing to be set the date of January 15 as the deadline for Iraq to pull out of Kuwait.

January 15 happened to be Dr. Martin Luther King, Jr.'s, birthday, the occasion for a national holiday to commemorate his life and message of nonviolence. Could Bush not have known? The linkage of King to the outbreak of the war, one day later, January 16, was ironic, but drew many blacks into the protests that followed.

The press, which had never adequately covered antiwar demonstrations to begin with, suddenly felt compelled to give equal time to flag-waving "support the troop" rallies going on daily. At one level it seemed fair. But at another, it was clear that what the "support the troops" rallies were simply echoing the party line emanating from the White House. The peace protesters, by contrast, had something different to say. They ended up largely unheard, however. To our great peril.

To capture the diverse flavor of these demonstrations and related activities and to stay on top of other war-related stories, we
began to run a column called "War and Peace." There was much
more going on than we could ever get into the column, but it was
a reminder that the war affected many people in many different
ways. After interviewing several leaders in the antiwar movement,
Martinez, at one point, asked me what lessons I took from the
1960s demonstrations. That question helped jar my thinking. All
week I had been wrestling with finding something to say that
would be useful and encouraging. Her question started me thinking about lessons I had learned from protesting the Vietnam War.
That led to other thoughts. I consulted with *NCR* Publisher Bill
McSweeney. We talked, as we often do about the overall direction
of the paper. I weighed some of his insights as well. What resulted
was an editorial containing 12 guiding points "to help us through
the days ahead." It was quickly dubbed: "Twelve steps to end U.S.
military addiction":

Where should peacemakers place their energies now that
the bombs are falling?

It is our judgment, one supported by most leaders of
most mainstream Christian denominations who have studied this conflict from both nonviolent and just-war traditions, that this war against Iraq is immoral.

We, along with millions of other Americans, feel outrage,
legitimate anger—much stemming from the profoundly sorrowful knowledge that this war was unnecessary. A conflict
of two presidents' egos has erupted into military warfare,
changing the course of history.

We must now promise one another our anger and sadness will not consume us, not demobilize us, not weaken
our resolve.

We offer the following 12 precepts as guides to help us
through the days ahead:

1. Prayer is foundational. We must begin and end our days in prayer, remembering we are, at best, instruments of God's peace. We will do what we can within our limits, stretching those limits, and ask God to do the rest.

Prayer protects us from burnout, leads us to proper judgments and can encourage us to live by the nonviolent teachings of Jesus preserved within our Christian churches.

2. Our concerns must be inclusive. We pray and care for the Israeli grandfather, the Iraqi mother, the U.S. fighter pilot or soldier in the sand. We pray for Presidents Bush and Hussein.

3. We must remind ourselves and our critics that true patriotism *can require* one to speak out against public policy, especially when one finds violations of justice, national ideals and human decency.

4. We must encourage communication with those who disagree with us. Desecration of national symbols, foremost the nation's flag, only alienates those whose hearts and minds we must reach.

5. As we press our nation's leaders to stop the carnage, we cannot oversimplify the complex realities of the Middle East or lose sight of the atrocities committed by Hussein. We must offer reasonable alternatives to the current course of U.S. military action. As we call for a cessation of the killing, we must reassert, for example, the need for a bolstered nonaligned U.N. peacekeeping force in the region.

6. We must continue to press our nation and others involved in the conflict to address *root issues*, including just Israeli security concerns and rightful demands by Palestinians for a homeland.

7. We must demand much better analysis in our media. We should ask for a wider variety of ideas on television. We

need deeper probes into the changing character of U.S. militarism and concurrent national-security mentality.

Some critical questions not yet addressed include: Why the pell-mell rush into this war? What economic and banking interests fueled this rush? Had secret promises been made to Saudi Arabia and Kuwait?

8. We must stress in our dialogue the practical consequences of war. We must show the connections between the billions spent on arms and the cutbacks in our neighborhoods. We must ask who is to pay for this war? How much will the inevitable 25-year U.S. troop commitment in the Middle East cost?

9. We must press our nation to develop energy policies that free us from dependence upon Middle East petroleum. This will require significant personal and national conservation measures. It will require the development of renewable energy systems. We cannot change national policy overnight, but we can by tomorrow personally pledge ourselves and our families to consume 25 percent less petroleum this year. This is, at base, an *oil war*.

10. We must support those who, through conscience, find they cannot fight in this war. We must educate our parishes to these and other peace issues, providing sanctuary if required.

11. We must financially support those peace and justice organizations dedicated to our common ideals. We can no longer take them for granted.

12. We must recognize that all this takes us into a resistance mode. Our nation's greedy consumption habits, its military idolatry, its jingoistic arrogance, its weakened free press, the purchase of elected representatives, secret government by an elite inner circle, all this must make us conscious that these are times demanding extraordinary responses. Know-

ing that these are extraordinary times can help clarify the path ahead.

We have come a distance in our generation. We have a long way to go. We must humbly remember we are always building, always serving to achieve a more just and peaceful world. Our contributions are never insignificant.

Dorothy Day, founder of the Catholic Worker movement, once said that "no one has a right to sit down and feel helpless. There's too much work to do."

We, with millions of others, are recommitting ourselves to the task.

Dorothy Day was right. No one has the right to sit down and feel helpless. We were pleased to have written an action-oriented editorial. We received many requests for permission to reprint and distribute this piece. We were happy to give it.

Another person I found very encouraging at the time was Benedictine Sister Joan Chittister, an *NCR* columnist, board member and good adviser. Chittister is articulate and visionary. She travels extensively and picks up what people are saying and doing. She will call me, often from an airport, to ask what she might write about in *NCR*. This particular week, we agreed that she would write about her personal struggle to come to terms with the morality of the war. She said she wanted to get beyond what might be viewed as a "knee-jerk liberal" opposition to the U.S. actions in the Gulf. The next day by fax came Chittister's column. She pointed to three problems she had with the war. First, the negative effect of force. Second, the war's capacity for desensitization. Third, its long term implications. Characteristically insightful, her essay is worth quoting at some length:

"There are three problems with this war. First is the problem of negative effect of force. Iraq is a country of 13 million people. Its economy is weak. Its people are poor. Its technology is limited. The United States is 20 times its size and wealth and development. Surely, the United States will "win."

But what will the win say in the world of runaway technology and unequal distribution of resources? Won't the win really say that the great and powerful have the right not to negotiate because they can solve problems the easy way? They can blast everybody else's questions to oblivion, obliterate their opposition, demolish their resistance. Won't the win really say that might does make right, that force is the answer to everything and that the powerful never have to sit down at the table to talk with the powerless?

Or, just as problematic, does being right give anyone the license to destroy the property or destroy the economy or destroy the culture or destroy the institutions of a people that in the end destroys their lives whether they die or not? The second problem with this war is its capacity for desensitization.

They are calling this the first full-scale technological war in history. What they mean is that it is inhuman, antiseptic, unreal, remote, "untouched by human hands." Baghdad never sees its enemy and the enemy never sees its victims. The enemy is an unmanned missile launched from carriers hundreds of miles away or supersonic jets too high or too fast to be spotted. Neither the crew on the ship nor the crew in the airplane ever hears the crash of the bombs or sees the fires they started, or watches the fine, imposing buildings being dynamited out of the heart of the city, or beholds the human faces of the little people who have been caught scurrying in the maelstrom.

Television reporters asked an Air Force colonel who had just returned from one of the 3,000 bombing runs in 14 hours, "What will you do now, colonel?" And he said, "Well, first I promised to buy my crew coffee. So we will have breakfast and then we'll get right back to work." Back to killing. Back to work.

And the rest of us watch the war in our living rooms for hours, eating and drinking like we do during the Super Bowl. This war, in other words, is making all of us a little less human. It is really killing everyone. The third problem with this war is the implications of it.

We have, apparently, given a great deal of thought to this war. The president, newscasters told us, worked on the 15-minute speech announcing the war two weeks before the deadline for starting it.

There has not been a word, however, about what we intend to do when it is over.

What shall we do with devastated country in social, economic and political turmoil? Will we do what we did with Panama and leave its innocent homeless in tents indefinitely?

Will we now provide a standing police force in the Middle East to wage the next war there? And who will pay for a war once estimated at $40 billion and now, just one week later, quickly rebudgeted to $100 billion in a country already too deeply in debt for day care or grants for education.

And how will we deal in a totally interconnected world, with a frustrated Arab population whose leaders may have given assent to Western forces on Muslim soil but whose people hate the infidel with a passion simple and profound?

What made the Iraq war different from all previous wars was television. Vietnam came to us on the evening news two decades ago. But that was before instant satellite hookups. Back then, television footage was rushed from the front lines to Saigon, where it was flown to Hong Kong to be uplifted to satellites over the Pacific in time to be edited and shown on the evening news. The process took a good part of a day—and that was considered fast compared with news-gathering in what now seems like the ancient international communications times, pre-satellite era.

During the Gulf War, live broadcasts were not all that was new. CNN's 24-hour headline news and around the clock coverage meant that every half-hour during the day—and often continuously—viewers had a chance to see and hear tragedy live in their living rooms. We became war voyeurs. Who can ever forget that first night when upstart CNN had a monopoly broadcasting the Baghdad bombings? Who can forget CNN's Bernard Shaw scrambling about his ninth-floor room in the Al-Rasheed Hotel in downtown Baghdad: "Ladies and Gentlemen, I've never been there, but it feels like we're in the center of hell." Who can forget the CNN crew in their Jerusalem bureau the following night speaking through gas masks before wobbling, hand-held cameras as sirens warned of another Iraqi Scud missile attack? Because of the difference between time zones, we were able to see it all during prime time, but we stayed up well into the night anyway.

Television has fastened humanity together as never before. Live broadcasts of coronations, state funerals, football and soccer games, Academy Award presentations—all have become shared world events for the global human family: secular communions. During the second evening of the bombing, I was watching television in my kitchen as I spoke on the telephone to my brother in Canberra, Australia, where it was early morning the next day. Suddenly, an incoming Scud missile exploded somewhere near Jerusalem and a camera caught the flash and smoke rising in the distant background. "Jim," I exclaimed, "a missile has just hit Israel!" "I know it. I see it!" he shot back. Clearly, television had revolutionized war.

It does not take much thought to realize that this powerful tool had become a major factor in influencing the course of modern warfare. From watching those early telecasts, we learned that the military planners at the Pentagon had given thought to the same subject. Those uncensored live broadcasts were to end soon, as press restrictions quickly grew and Israeli, Iraqi and U.S. military censors assumed the upper hand. In theory, it was argued, the censorship was needed to keep vital information from getting into enemy hands. But the restrictions became so severe that it became clear to most in the media that what was going on was war management, plain and simple.

No doubt, the Pentagon was acting on the assumption that if the American public were to actually see suffering and death, it would weaken popular support for the war.

They were probably right.

Fortunately, television *can* cause us to enter into the sufferings of other people and to respond to those sufferings. This, I have always felt, is a blessing. It even offers the possibility that our nation, in so many ways cut off from so much of the rest of the world's hunger and pain, might someday come to better appreciate the way most of the planet live—and die.

On the second day of the bombings, we decided we needed someone with a good media understanding to write about the war as it was reaching us through television. Jesuit Father Raymond Schroth, journalism professor at Loyola University in New Orleans and an *NCR* contributor, quickly agreed to sit in front of the tube for *NCR* and watch the war. His piece in the February 1 issue was the first of three he was to file during the war. His comments on what we were being shown are among the best to be found anywhere in the press for that period. It did not take long, once we had received his first file, to decide that this was front-page material. The following are excerpts from his article:

A resident adviser in one of our college dorms tells me his students watched the CNN live war the first day and cheered and took bets as if they were watching a football game. Small wonder. A sports mind-set has revved us up for the war. Some weeks ago, TV's most disconcerting image was of Defense Secretary Dick Cheney whipping the cheering troops into a fighting frenzy as if he were a coach at half time in a locker room.

A pilot back from bombing Baghdad descends from his fighter-bomber and says, "I just went in there and scored my touchdown!" A father glued to the screen sees his son land and wave to the cameras. "It's like I had a ringside seat," he says. . . .

On Thursday evening's CBS "Showdown in the Gulf," Dan Rather promises to show us Saddam Hussein "hunkered down in his bunker." We're no doubt meant to recall who else ended his days in a bunker. . . .

Switch to the White House. George Bush is up early and chats with aides in a doorway. Still shots of Bush on the phone with world leaders. Bush at prayer service organized by Billy Graham. No image-tailoring here. . . .

On the local religious cable channel, shared by EWTN, the Catholic Cable Network and a Protestant fundamentalist group, Los Angeles Archbishop Roger Mahony appears in a brief spot to say in English and in Spanish that he prayerfully hopes the troops will return from the Gulf without having to use force.

"Why doesn't he tell us it's an unjust war?" I ask. . . .

Ironically, the ultimate value of TV coverage was not in its visual images. For after the first day, they were nearly all selected for us by the Pentagon. Nor in its breadth and depth of information. For *The New York Times* and the other good newspapers certainly surpassed TV in their documentation. But in its occasional flashes of intellect, moments when commentators or GIs—like the one who told CBS, after launching a rocket, that it was "scary thinking of the damage done and lives lost"—said something that might make viewers think.

Like Mark Shield's just rage at the establishment, who send their compliments to the "volunteer army" but not their children to fight the war. And the guest journalist on "MacNeil/Lehrer" who called the war a video game staged to make us forget what war is really about, an appalling high-tech bloody exercise that shouldn't happen."

The high point for me came the first night . . . when "The Killing Fields" Sydney Schanberg, who has seen war up close, barely able to control his anger, leaned forward and asked Rep. Stephen Solarz, who is running for secretary of state on this issue and has not seen war up close—asked him how he educated himself on the "terribleness of war" before he attempted to lead Congress into its declaration.

Solarz had no answer. Desperate, he fell back on invoking the Holocaust—wrapping it around him like the "patriotic" coward simply invokes the flag.

Schanberg told me in a telephone interview later that all we can gain from war is to try to learn something—although we have been slow to learn so far. The role of the press, he said, is to witness the war on behalf of the nation, to be the people's eyes at the front, to force us to truly consider the "terribleness" of war so that we are responsible for what we do.

Tragically, because of perhaps the tightest censorship in history, we don't have those eyes there now. . . ."

There was so much we did not know. So much that was being kept from us. What Pentagon studies, what White House "findings," what covert-action decisions were being kept from the American people by those with "national security" mentalities? The problem, of course, is that democracy cannot function in the dark. Wars—and Iraq provides a prime example—have a tendency to chip away at basic freedoms and weaken democracies. The question I kept asking myself was, would enough people show enough concern early enough to keep the "democratic experiment" alive?

There was also much we did not understand about the people we were warring with. Nor did our leaders seem to care about understanding Islamic culture and religion. This was also dangerous. We *all* needed to know more about Islam—and in a hurry. At the paper, we were ready to do what we could. We were just about ready to give birth to a project we had been working on for many months, a special issue on Islam. It was set for the following week.

5

Inside Islam

During the Vietnam War, nothing bothered me more than hearing Americans say, "Life is cheap in Asia." The words became part of casual conversations so frequently that they became accepted as reality and were rarely disputed. But this was wrong. Life was not "cheap" in Vietnam. Every mother I had seen lose a son grieved as much as any mother I knew back home in the United States. In Vietnam, when a picture was available, the dead son's image would be placed on the family altar shrine next to other deceased family members. The pain was real. That the young die more frequently in the world's poor nations, lacking in adequate food and medicine, only means mothers there must endure these losses more often than other women.

It is sad to see Americans ascribe to poverty's victims a diminished value of life. I have often wondered whether this might be part of an effort to protect our consciences, especially when the U.S. military is the cause of those deaths.

No, life is not "cheap in Asia." It is precious there like it is everywhere else. Life is irreplaceable. It could even be argued that, among the world's poor, who have virtually no support outside the family, life assumes an even greater value than we are likely to appreciate in the West. For the poor, each family loss adds to the threat of one's own survival. I say this because these thoughts were on my mind when I decided after the beginning of the Middle East buildup that we must try to do some fresh reporting on Middle East culture, in particular the Islamic religion.

After some discussion with the staff, we decided to publish a "primer" on Islam, a special pullout section on Islamic-Christian relations. *NCR's* opening into the Middle East is obviously through religion. Reporting on Islam made sense.

The late historian Christopher Dawson wrote that religion shapes culture. To understand a culture, he would say, study its religion. We developed a plan that led to a series of reports and essays on Islam for our February 8 issue. *NCR* staff writer Demetria Martinez examined Islam in the United States, especially its growth among black Americans. Eastern Europe correspondent Tim McCarthy, then in Prague, flew to Istanbul, center of ancient Middle East religious life, to interview key ecumenists. George Irani, a Lebanese-born Catholic living in Indiana, coordinated the editing of several articles on Christian-Islamic relations. Managing editor Dawn Gibeau, working with Irani, designed and put the final touches on the primer. Meanwhile, Vatican affairs writer Peter Hebblethwaite wrote an essay tracing the history of Catholic-Islamic relations through the centuries. In the end, the entire effort filled almost half an issue.

It was our intention to treat Islam objectively, but also sympathetically. We wanted to get below the stereotypes to understand how Muslims looked at themselves and their world, as well as to document the work going on toward improving Christian and Islamic relations in the Middle East and elsewhere. If the past were any indicator, we suspected the primer would be especially helpful for high-school and college teachers. For example, it contained important dates in 20th-century Islam as well as key concepts in the Islamic religion. It also contained addresses of groups involved in Islamic-Christian dialogue, examples of English words derived from Arabic (e.g., alcohol, candy, jar and sugar), a map showing where and in what numbers Muslims lived in the Middle East and, finally, a bibliography for further reading.

I knew that to succeed in this project I would need to rely on outside advisers. I certainly claim no personal expertise in the region. It is not uncommon for an editor to go outside his or her

publication for help. As for *NCR*, I have found that the church provides a ready network of willing and able advisers on virtually any
topic one can imagine. As it turned out, my principle Middle East
adviser was Irani, a professor at Franklin College in Franklin, Indiana. Bright, sensitive, Irani is a valuable link between two cultures.
At times, as the Islam issue developed, we spoke daily by phone.
The excerpts below provide some flavor of the newspaper's Islamic issue. More of it appears in the appendix.

McCarthy's piece from Istanbul captured some of the mood of a
Middle East city at the time of the war. It showed how the conflict
had added to religious tensions in the area:

> . . . Today, with war howling round the Persian Gulf,
> much history still swings on that Bosporus hinge, a strip of
> water between Europe and Asia that a strong swimmer
> could stroke without a pause. Less than a week before war
> erupted, few people here thought it would ever happen. As
> a local merchant put it, "Whoever heard of a war starting
> by appointment?" Those were the Turks. The Europeans
> and Americans were less certain.
>
> One of those Americans was Melvin Wittler, Middle East
> general secretary for the United Church Board for World
> Ministry. The board, known here as Amerikan Bord, oper-
> ates three college preparatory schools and a publishing
> house (Redhouse Press) in Turkey. Wittler has been in Is-
> tanbul for 35 years and knows the region well.
>
> A few days before the United Nations' Jan. 15 deadline
> for Saddam Hussein to pull out of Kuwait, Wittler, an ur-
> bane, soft-spoken man, sat in his Istanbul office and de-
> scribed how relations with the Muslims had improved since
> he first came to the city in the 1950s. If war comes, he said,
> it will obviously have an effect upon Christians in Turkey,
> but the effect will be most severe in the southeastern part of
> the country, near the border with Iraq. Istanbul, after all, is

more than 800 miles from Baghdad. About a week later, on Jan. 22, Wittler's office was bombed.

A Turkish left-wing group claimed responsibility for the attack, in protest against American imperialism rather than Christianity, but the point holds. No quake rocks these ancient lands without sending tremors through Istanbul.

East/West, rich/poor, democracy/dictatorship, secular/religious, these dichotomies and more meet at this world crossroad and the tensions they generate have earned this city its age-old reputation for intrigue.

Last December, the following letter went out to all Istanbul shops that had decorated their windows for Christmas: "Dear Shop Owner: By decorating your shop window, you are supporting Christmas, which is accepted as the birthday of Jesus and celebrated by all the Christian world. We urge you to give up this wish. Or else you will be punished by death in the face of justice."

The letter was reportedly sent by the Iranian-backed Hezbollah Party and the threat was not idle. Last year there were 24 assassinations in Turkey, many of them religiously motivated. They included journalist Turan Dursun, a former clergyman, and secularist theologian Bahriye Üçok, a champion of women's rights. None of the killers has been caught, and critics charge that Islamic fundamentalists have infiltrated the police force as well as the government. . . .

Wrote Tamara Sonn, director of the international studies program at St. John Fisher College in Rochester, New York:

At an interfaith dialogue recently in Rochester, N.Y., participants were asked to identify the tradition represented in the following quote: "The covenant between God and humanity requires that we establish a society on earth that reflects the equality we all share in the eyes of God."

The Jews, the Christians and the Muslims present each claimed the sentiment represented their own faiths, though in fact it is from the great Pakistani scholar of Islam, Fazlur Rahman, who died in 1987.

The purpose of the exercise was to demonstrate the similarity—indeed, virtual identity—of ethical standards shared by the three "children of Abraham."

Ihsan A. Bagby, director of Islamic education at the Islamic Teaching Center in Plainfield, Indiana, wrote:

Today (in the United States), there are . . . 1,061 mosques and places of prayer—a remarkable 1,400 percent increase (since the 1960s). In 1960 there were no full-time Islamic schools; today, there are 65 full-time schools. From a total below half a million in 1960, the number of Muslims has risen by conservative estimates to four million. This total makes Islam larger than most Christian denominations.

Researchers Dr. Martin Marty of the University of Chicago and Dr. Yvonne Haddad of the University of Massachusetts predict that Muslims will be the second-largest religion in America soon after 2000 A.D.

Wrote Irani:

. . . Of the 22 Arab countries that are members of the Arab League, Lebanon is the only one to have a Christian president of the republic.

For the Vatican, Lebanon, with its 17 communities—Christian and Muslim—represents the ideal testing ground for true coexistence between religions.

Wrote Hebblethwaite:

The motive behind the Crusades was not just to bash the Muslims. The first impulse was ecumenical: The Byzantine emperor, Alexius I Comnenus, had asked for papal help.

(Pope) Urban (II) wanted to heal the schism of 1054. It had not yet hardened into irrevocability.

Among Urban's ecumenical advisers was St. Anselm, archbishop of Canterbury. They were together at the rather leisurely siege of Capua in northern Italy.

Observers note the contrast between the splendidly caparisoned tent of the pope, to which only the rich and powerful were admitted, and Anselm's improvised tent where everyone was welcome, including the *pagani* or Muslims who had come from Sicily to join in the siege. . . .

It was such conversations with Muslims that led Anselm to write his treatise, *Cur Deus Homo* (why God became man). It was and remains the most fundamental question. Anselm's witness is important: Even at the time of the first Crusade, there were Christians who offered an alternative religious approach to the military solution.

We concluded the issue with an editorial that outlines some of the social and cultural questions we felt needed greater examination. The following excerpts are taken from that editorial:

. . . Outsiders wanting to live at peace with or have any lasting influence upon foreign cultures must first understand them; second, respect them; and third, work within their identities, values and myths.

These are essential requirements for civil conduct and have become more critical for human survival as the world, through jet transport and electronic communication, becomes increasingly a "global village." Western technologies have united us with the East and Middle East but have far outpaced our abilities to understand the new responsibilities these linkages entail.

By any measure, the Middle East offers a complex landscape where tribal, political and religious factors are prominent and not easily understood. Most of the countries of the Arab Middle East today are only 40 years old. . . .

Most of these sheikdoms in the Gulf are, at best, precarious and artificial national creations. They are united by culture and history more than by national identity. "Our" Arabs today, meanwhile, are those who hold the purses and control the oil prices. They are the House of Saud in Saudi Arabia and the Sabah family in Kuwait. With their huge fortunes, they have purchased U.S. military power to defend them. However, this power alone will almost certainly not be enough to maintain stability in these countries. . . .

Further and importantly, the Palestinian question is still today an ongoing drama nagging the consciousness of all Arabs and Muslims in general. Bush and his aides are better advised to devise a viable solution to the Arab-Israeli-Palestinian problem if they want to see lasting stability in the Middle East.

If this reality does not seep into Bush's mind, then no air sorties or carpet-bombing will be enough to bring a "new order" to the Middle East. Any new order cannot be husbanded apart from a sensible knowledge of the Arab and Muslim popular concerns and hopes. Christians and Muslims have tall orders to fill, but it is never too late.

During the war, I was keenly aware of how little most of us know about the Middle East. Former Kennedy administration adviser and historian Arthur Schlesinger, Jr., in a *New York Times* commentary critical of Bush's Middle East policies, amplified the point: Ignorance is not the problem, he said. The problem is being ignorant of one's own ignorance.

Ignorance can be lethal. In the case of the Middle East, it certainly is. The Gulf War has shown us precisely this. It was apparent, after only a week or two, that the bombings were leading to the collapse of Iraqi society and fueling centuries-old ethnic and religious hostilities. It seemed Bush's policies were going to cause a power vacuum likely to lead to new encroachments from Iran, whose Shiite religious followers were more hostile to the West than Iraq's largely Sunni population. Further, the Kurds along the Turkish border, eager to do war with Hussein, had intentions of their own. But would the U.S. ally, Turkey, with its own restless Kurds, tolerate these new expressions of autonomy? Much was uncertain. It seemed Bush had not thought through the possible consequences of his policies and did not seek advice from academics familiar with the Middle East. Bush's bombs were setting into motion a complex chain of events almost certain to produce long-term bloodshed. The outcome of it all seemed only to heighten the probability that the region would become even more hostile to the United States than it had been before the war. All of us knew so little. Our special issue on Islam was a small step toward remedying that fact.

6

Peace Morality

At one level, the Iraq war was a good news—bad news tale. The good news was that at crucial moments, both before and during the Gulf War, many pressing moral questions were being asked and with an unprecedented intensity. The bad news, from a Christian perspective, was that many critical questions were not being asked of the Bush administration. This was largely the result of President Bush's adroit use of the media (which, from all appearances, was generally willing to be used) and many U.S. church leaders' failure to confront popular sentiment. The administration co-opted the discussions. Bush became prosecuting attorney, judge and juror in the U.S. court of moral law by first framing the ethical issues to his maximum benefit and then passing judgment on them.

The U.S. public was generally eager to affirm its belief that it was acting morally. Unwilling, as ever, to examine the darker, more selfish side of its character, it agreeably went along with Bush once it had been more or less promised few American casualties. For a U.S. administration, this became a textbook case on how to win an overseas war at home. For U.S. church leaders, the U.S. bishops included, it represented a serious setback—even as it provided sobering lessons—on the long road to build peace churches and to weave nonviolence and peaceful conflict resolution into the wider public values. Only the religious organizations, it seems to me, can turn the nation from its idolatry of the war course to rediscover its proper place in the human family.

To get a handle on what began to be called "the just-war de-bate" (and the way *NCR* saw it and reported on it), we need to begin at the Christian beginning. It needs to be said at the outset that Jesus never spoke of a "just war." This passage from Luke (6:27-36) is straightforward:

> But I tell you who hear me: Love your enemies, do good to those who hate you, bless those who curse you, and pray for those who mistreat you. If anyone hits you on one cheek, let him hit the other one too; if someone takes your coat, let him have your shirt as well. Give to everyone who asks you for something, and when someone takes what is yours, do not ask for it back. Do for others just what you want them to do for you.
>
> If you love only the people who love you, why should you receive a blessing? Even sinners love those who love them! And if you do good only to those who do good to you, why should you receive a blessing? Even sinners do that! And if you lend only to those from whom you hope to get it back, why should you receive a blessing? Even sinners lend to sinners, to get back the same amount! No! Love your enemies and do good to them; lend and expect nothing back. You will then have a great reward, and you will be sons and daughters of the Most High God. For God himself is good to the ungrateful and wicked. Be merciful just as your Father is merciful.

Throughout the first three centuries of church history, the church taught Christian pacifism. Many Christians went to their deaths rather than take up swords in battle. But with the fourth century came Constantine and Christianity, when a religion of rebels and renegades became the official religion of the empire. The church gradually abandoned its antiwar posture. It began to accommodate war, or rather, "just wars." In the fifth century, when St. Augustine formulated his just-war theory, bows and arrows were the current high-tech weaponry. Most fighting was still done with swords and spears. In the context of that kind of war-making,

Augustine argued that wars are believed to be wrong unless certain criteria are met.

These included:

1. that war be declared by a legitimate authority;
2. that it be a last resort;
3. that it have a good intention;
4. that it allow for the protection of the innocent;
5. that the proportion of good over evil be kept.

Over the centuries, other thinkers refined these conditions, yet the just-war theory remained the dominant theory on war in the Christian tradition.

The problem with the theory, however, was that rather than providing an effective impediment to war, it more often became the gateway to battle. At best, it could be argued that in theory the analysis was useful in limiting the scope of warfare, but, in practice, wars tended to be fought to their technical limits. Frequently, the just-war theory was used by both sides in a conflict. Both the French and German bishops, for example, invoked the theory during World War II to exhort their citizens to battle.

After World War II, Pope Pius XII spoke out against the terrifying new weapons of war. In his 1944 Christmas message, for example, he called upon the world to "reject modern warfare with its monstrous means of conducting hostilities." With the birth of the atomic age, the Catholic Church began to look more seriously at the consequences of modern warfare. The world went to the "brink" twice, once over Berlin, once over Cuba. Then in 1963, Pope John XXIII, in his encyclical, "Peace On Earth," argued that the arms race and warfare violated the natural order and that they represented a denial of the unity of the human family. This was, then, the real awakening of the church to a more serious reevaluation necessitated by the awesome buildup of nuclear weapons by the superpowers, principally the United States and Soviet Union.

The 1965 Vatican Council document, "The Constitution on the Church in the Modern World," was to add to the urgency of the discussion, calling for "an evaluation of war with an entirely new attitude." Again, the document stressed the solidarity of the human family and the threat of nuclear weapons and stated specifically that "any act of war, aimed indiscriminately at the destruction of entire cities or extensive areas along with their population, is a crime against God and man himself. It merits unequivocal and unhesitating condemnation." Importantly, a move had begun away from just-war thinking and toward framing war discussions into a context that stressed the nature of the human family and the role of Christians as peacemakers. Many Catholic moralists throughout the church would pick up these themes in the years that followed. But through the decades, the nuclear arsenals continued to grow. With the advent of intercontinental nuclear missiles and multiple warheads, the stakes grew perilously higher as the "response time"—that desperately brief time between first launch and retaliatory decision—dropped to a matter of minutes. By 1980 the nuclear powers had assembled weapons with an equivalent firepower of at least one million Hiroshima bombs. The problem became increasingly apparent. Proliferating weapons of massive destruction were defying human imagination and escaping convincing moral assessment. Understandably, one might not have expected such an assessment at the time within the Soviet Union, but what about within the United States, where freedom of speech has been a celebrated tradition? Shouldn't the U.S. bishops, as moral leaders, feel compelled to speak their minds.

Clearly, some bishops felt they must. It took only one, Auxiliary Bishop Francis J. Murphy of Baltimore, to tip the first domino. Many other bishops were more than willing to critique the "my-country-right-or-wrong" approach to U.S. war-making. Among them was Thomas J. Gumbleton, auxiliary bishop of Detroit, later described in an *NCR* profile as a "combative pacifist," alluding to his fierce, hockey-playing style.

Murphy introduced a new item on the agenda, for the National Conference of Catholic Bishops' November 1980 annual meeting in Washington, calling on the bishops' conference to produce "a concise summary of the church's teaching on war and peace" that would lead to a "strong educational effort on those issues within the church." The quotations are from a 1983 book by *NCR* contributor Jim Castelli, *The Bishops and the Bomb: Waging Peace in a Nuclear Age.*

The *NCR* national affairs editor at the time, Patty Edmonds, wrote of that meeting: "Several bishops rose to plead that the bishops study and speak on the issue (of war and peace, with special emphasis on the arms race); Detroit Auxiliary Gumbleton was the last. "We have just elected a (U.S.) president (Ronald Reagan)," he said, "who has sincerely stated that we can have superiority with nuclear weapons, and a vice president (George Bush) who has said we can fight a nuclear war and win it. We now have to face the question clearly; we have to responsibly repeat what Pope John Paul suggested in his Peace Day message: 'Violence is not the Catholic way; violence is not the way of Jesus'."

Gumbleton was highly visible as an ad hoc committee member. He had been visible in Christmas 1980 when he traveled to Iran to pray with U.S. hostages; he would be visible again, 10 years later, in Baghdad, praying with different hostages as he attempted to lend his influence to seeing them freed.

Gumbleton traces his pacifist leanings to the Berrigan brothers, Thomas Merton's writings, his friendship with pacifist Gordon Zahn and from Dorothy Day's Catholic Worker nonviolence beliefs.

In another way, the Detroit auxiliary was simply one of those bishops at the forefront as a church of 19th-century immigrants—grateful immigrants, not practiced in criticizing the nation's war policies—shifted position. These immigrants had been the backbone of U.S. anticommunism through the middle years of the 20th century. Therefore, to stand up and criticize, let alone condemn, some established national policy verged on heresy. The same situation still existed when the Iraq-U.S. conflict began—most Catholics have not absorbed the enormous shift that has taken place in their church, from papal and episcopal sources, on war and war-making.

But the peace pastoral and Gulf War opposition had their episcopal roots with such bishops as Gumbleton, the late Memphis Bishop Carroll T. Dozier and Richmond, Virginia, Bishop Walter Sullivan, who had gained support in the late 1970s through the quiet ground swell of U.S. Catholic peace activists. Those activists were frequently people gathering and sharing information and views as part of the U.S. branch of the international Catholic peace movement, Pax Christi U.S.A. In the mid-1970s, the annual meeting of Pax Christi could be held comfortably in a small classroom. By the early 1980s, hundreds would come from throughout the United States to hear speakers and to share literature in the burgeoning field of Catholic peace literature.

Murphy's call led to the formation of a five-member committee of U.S. bishops, headed by Chicago Archbishop Joseph Bernardin and eventually, through several draft revisions, lengthy consultations and deliberations involving tens of thousands of U.S. Catholics, to the May 3,1983, publication of "The Challenge of Peace: God's Promise and Our Response," informally known as the U.S. bishops' peace pastoral.

It was a heady, divisive and even frightening time in U.S. Catholic history. Heady because the subjects were as pressing and critical as any moral issues the bishops had ever faced. Divisive because the country was not ready for a serious discussion on the morality of nuclear weapons—the bishops had to force open the door. And frightening because what the bishops would finally say, many thought, could even spell the difference between survival and annihilation. Who was to stand in the way of what appeared to many to be a mad rush to self-destruction? Only a body as prominent as the U.S. bishops, many thought, had the necessary credentials.

It was about this time that I became editor of *NCR*. I came just as the 1980s were under way. I had been an editor at the *Washing-*

ton Star and earlier a reporter for five years at the *Detroit Free Press* after returning from Vietnam in December 1972. Jason Petosa, then the publisher, and Arthur Jones, the editor, had asked me to write a letter saying what I expected to do at the paper. Among many ideas, I stressed my intention to emphasize the nuclear weapons issue. In June 1980 I moved into my new post. Within months, we had stories about nuclear weapons and weapons proliferation as well as numerous statements on the subject by moralists.

One chagrined *NCR* colleague counted 26 separate references to nuclear weapons in one issue of the newspaper and asked, "Isn't that a bit much?" Another *NCR* colleague, describing the paper under Fox, the new editor, summed it up in three words: "nukes, nukes, nukes." It was a passion, but I was not alone in following the passion. Our coverage complemented the growing concern in the churches in the early 1980s. Through three drafts, and against open opposition from the Reagan White House and the U.S. military establishment, the bishops worked on their peace pastoral. Finally, in Chicago, on May 3, 1983, the bishops voted 238-9 to commit the church to peace. My editorial that day would speak to issues raised by the Iraq war eight years later. The following is from the editorial that appeared that week (May 13, 1983):

> Despite the document's shortcomings, it could well be the most important religious statement of our time. This is not because of any single insight or particular line of reasoning contained in the pastoral, but rather because at long last moral analysis can no longer be ignored as an essential element in any discussion of nuclear strategies.

> The bishops have forced the issue.

> Many are beginning to understand this. A group of scientists and defense experts, for example, last week congratulated the bishops for their work and for "reintroducing concepts of moral philosophy and ethics into the analysis of

what's right and what's wrong with our thinking and actions concerning nuclear weapons and war. . . ."

The time is late, but not too late. The pastoral is one more visible sign that the time has come to reverse the arms race. What has been required is a breakthrough from a self-destructive mentality which believes that somehow ever more deadly weapons are needed to avert nuclear confrontation. But history has taught a different lesson: weapons, once produced, are eventually used. The bishops' pastoral, by calling for an emphatic "halt" to nuclear escalation, is aimed at producing that breakthrough. . . .

The question still outstanding is this: How much will Christians be willing to risk to carry out these new commitments?

From the outset, *NCR* has supported the bishops' efforts to develop a strong peace pastoral. After two years of work, the fruit of the bishops' work is not all we had hoped it would be. We have, for example, serious reservations about including in the statement an even "strictly conditioned acceptance" of nuclear deterrence. The bishops believe such an acceptance is justifiable—but only as a step toward true disarmament.

But we have argued that history since Hiroshima shows deterrence brings only further escalation. We have further argued for the condemnation of the very possession of nuclear weapons which exist only to terrorize or kill. And we regret how far so much of the pastoral has strayed from early Christian teaching to love those who would do you harm and to put down the sword even if it means taking up the cross.

Nonviolent alternatives need further exploration. It is our hope that this peace pastoral will serve as a springboard for further thought and discussion in this area.

Our greatest fear—one realized with the publication of the third draft—had been that in the process of refining moral arguments, the bishops would water down important moral concepts and be co-opted by national policymakers— be they in the United States or abroad. Ambiguous phrases and the inclusion of the word "curb" in its reference to the arms race seriously weakened the document. U.S. officials used that ambiguity in the third draft to claim the bishops as gentle allies. . . .

Tens of thousands have contributed to the pastoral. They have spoken out, written their bishops, lit candles and whispered prayers. The bishops, meanwhile, listened well, attempting to represent their dioceses while staying in step with Vatican teachings. The process has been largely open and the church has changed positively as a result. The bishops came under fire from those who wanted to steer them away from war and peace politics; but undaunted, they quietly continued their work, fully aware that some moral teachings are bound to have political consequences. Lessons have been learned, and these have been solid gains.

Two more points are linked to this pastoral and its applicability to the U.S. war with Iraq. The first is the attitude of the chairman of the bishops' Ad Hoc Committee on War and Peace toward what the bishops were about. Chicago Cardinal Joseph Bernardin opened the first committee meeting on July 26, 1981, by explaining that the committee's genesis and its mandate was "to take a new look at war."

As the Iraq confrontation grew into armed conflict, that is precisely what *NCR* was attempting to do: to take a new look at the war enveloping us.

The second point is to remind ourselves that the bishops were not simply concerned with nuclear weapons. On the contrary, they saw arms sales and conventional weapons as independent triggers of death, as well as triggers that can spark the greater confrontation. The following is from the U.S. bishops' peace pastoral (paragraphs 209-214):

> While it is right and proper that priority be given to reducing and ultimately eliminating the likelihood of nuclear war, this does not of itself remove the threat of other forms of warfare. Indeed, negotiated reduction in nuclear weapons available to the superpowers could conceivably increase the danger of nonnuclear wars.
>
> a) Because of this we strongly support negotiations aimed at reducing and limiting conventional forces and at building confidence between possible adversaries, especially in regions of potential military confrontations. We urge that prohibitions outlawing the production and use of chemical and biological weapons be reaffirmed and observed. Arms control negotiations must take account of the possibility that conventional conflict could trigger the nuclear confrontation the world must avoid.
>
> b) Unfortunately, as is the case with nuclear proliferation, we are witnessing a relaxation of restraints in the international commerce in conventional arms. Sales of increasingly sophisticated military aircraft, missiles, tanks, antitank weapons, antipersonnel bombs, and other systems by the major supplying countries (especially the Soviet Union, the United States, France, and Great Britain) have reached unprecedented levels.

Pope John Paul II took specific note of the problem in his U.N. address:

> The production and sale of conventional weapons throughout the world is a truly alarming and evidently growing phenomenon. . . . Moreover the traffic in these weapons seems to be developing at an increasing rate and seems to be directed most of all toward developing countries.

It is a tragic fact that U.S. arms sales policies in the last decade have contributed significantly to the trend the Holy Father deplores. We call for a reversal of this course. The United States should renew earlier efforts to develop multilateral controls on arms exports, and should in this case also be willing to take carefully chosen independent initiatives to restrain the arms trade. Such steps would be particularly appropriate where the receiving government faces charges of gross and systematic human rights violations. . . .

Tragically, just after the bishops published their remarks, the superpowers initiated yet another round of deadly Middle East weapons exports. These continued unabated to the eve of the Iraq war.

During those early years of the 1980s, I held the hope, however slim, that the superpowers might listen to the growing public rejection of armaments. It was during that period that bishop after U.S. bishop began to issue pastoral letters on the nuclear threat. Archbishops John Quinn of San Francisco and John Roach of St. Paul-Minneapolis, Bishops Leroy Matthiesen of Amarillo, Maurice Dingman of Des Moines, Francis Murphy of Baltimore, and Anthony Pilla of Cleveland all wrote important statements. But none captured national attention as much as an address by Archbishop Raymond Hunthausen of Seattle in July 1981 at the Pacific Northwest Synod of the Lutheran Church of America. Quoting an article titled "It's a Sin to Build a Nuclear Weapon," written by Jesuit pacifist Father Richard McSorley, Hunthausen said: "I agree. Our willingness to destroy life everywhere on this earth for the sake of our security as Americans is at the root of many other terrible events in our country." Hunthausen avoided the well-worn path of weighing the evils of nuclear weapons against just-war principles. Instead, he spoke the clear and simple language of the Gospels. "We are told . . . by our Lord: Blessed are the peacemakers. They shall be called the children of God." To be a peacemaker today, the Seattle archbishop said, is to accept the cross and consequences of persecution. Hunthausen called upon the U.S. leadership to begin unilateral disarmament, saying "we must dismantle our weapons of terror and place our reliance on God."

He called the Seattle area Trident base "the Auschwitz of Puget Sound" and he asked Christians to begin taking risks on behalf of peace and disarmament. "I would like to share a vision of still another action that could be taken," he said, "simply this—a sizable number of people in the state of Washington, 5,000, 10,000, 500,000 people, refusing to pay 50 percent of their taxes in nonviolent resistance to nuclear murder and suicide." Hunthausen had gone beyond merely deploring the state of affairs to call Christians to active resistance. He became the episcopal patron of a rapidly growing Catholic peace movement, giving hope to many who felt the church was still moving too slowly in confronting the evils of the U.S. nuclear buildup. His call would echo throughout the 1980s as his challenge considerably extended the reach of the Catholic peace movement, providing new legitimacy to acts of resistance. Hunthausen and the 1983 bishops' peace pastoral provided the model by which many Christian peace efforts through the 1980s would take shape and find their measure.

As the 1990s were under way and the Iraq imbroglio moved toward and then broke into open conflict, it was bishops' words and activists' actions that I often kept in mind. And it was these two groups I most often had before me as I tried to find the words—and articles—that would keep us focused on a reality that was muffled under the drums of war.

In some ways the U.S.-led war against Iraq caught many church leaders by surprise. While their peacemaking initiatives were far more pronounced during the 1980s than at any other time in U.S. history, their emphasis had been aimed at assessing, criticizing and condemning nuclear weapons and nuclear proliferation. As the Cold War thawed and Soviet and U.S. diplomats began working to cut strategic nuclear weapons by one-third (from 12,000 U.S weapons to, say, 8,000 and from 9,000 Soviet weapons to, say, 6,000!), the buildup of conventional weapons, their growing firepower and sales overseas, was receiving far too little public scrutiny or moral assessment.

By the 1990s, if war were to break out in any region of the world, the United States and a dozen other nations would be seen to have armed that region to the hilt, far beyond any of the local countries' rational defensive military needs. However, the linkage between armaments as a significant cause of warfare, and war itself breaking out, was rarely being raised as an issue for ethical consideration.

By November 1990, when the U.S. bishops met for their annual meeting, the bishops themselves were well-primed to discuss the morality of war. Iraq, however, was not on their agenda. It was quickly placed there, in the four-day meeting's opening hours, by Los Angeles Archbishop Roger Mahony, head of the bishops' international policy committee. In the previous decade, the U.S. Catholic bishops had shown increased self-assurance in addressing national security issues. Mahony had shown it over Iraq: five days before the bishops' gathering, the Los Angeles archbishop had sent to Secretary of State James Baker a letter outlining Catholic teaching on a "just war" as it applied to a possible U.S. war with Iraq.

With this as backdrop, on November 12, Mahony stood in front of his assembled colleagues and asked his fellow bishops to make his letter to Baker their own. What happened next was captured and reported in *NCR*'s November 23 issue. It offers a flavor of the give and take among the bishops and highlights their different approaches when confronted by a pressing military question:

> He (Mahony) wanted them "to affirm" what he had written, but many of them wanted more. "This is not the time to be timid," said Juneau, Alaska, Bishop Michael Kenny, who had just returned from Iraq with four ailing U.S. hostages. Insisted Kenny, "We are poised on the brink of a catastrophic war," and he warned of the potential for use of tactical nuclear weapons if a war started. Anchorage Arch-

bishop Francis Hurley urged a new conference statement. Boston Cardinal (Bernard) Law opposed it. Other bishops joined the debate, including New York Cardinal John O'Connor, a retired rear admiral. O'Connor urged the conference to add to Mahony's letter to Baker. O'Connor said the enormous expenditures required to finance operation "Desert Shield" took away from vital domestic needs such as housing the homeless and helping the poor. Pushed to a vote, however, Hurley's motion failed. A vote to support Mahony's letter was taken. It passed.

As a follow up to the vote, it was proposed that Mahony's committee lead the bishops "in a more detailed discussion" of questions surrounding the Persian Gulf crisis. Law, however, then stood up and, in effect, closed the doors by offering a motion (later passed on a written ballot) that all further Iraqi discussion take place behind closed doors. In discussions closed to the public, Law was the first to jump to his feet, urging the president of the bishops' conference, Cincinnati Archbishop Daniel E. Pilarczyk, not to send any letter. Law argued that a letter showing episcopal division on the Persian Gulf could weaken Bush's hand and play into that of Saddam Hussein. Law said he would publicly disassociate himself from any such letter sent. Law has not concealed from his fellow bishops his close association with Bush or with White House Chief of Staff John Sununu.

Many bishops thought Law's political instincts had derailed what otherwise could have been a healthy public moral discussion on the then looming Gulf War. Instead, bishops who had bravely and openly discussed and written about the crucial U.S. role in world peace, faced with a practical application of their teaching, felt it necessary to hide their legitimate and telling divisions.

The ludicrousness of their decision was apparent by the following week, by which time a virtual national debate on the Gulf had erupted on nightly television talk shows. U.S. bishops, such as Gumbleton and Mahony, had already been seen airing their views on network television; many bishops were pressed to appear locally in their dioceses to voice their views.

NCR editorialized November 23:

> The "executivizing" of last week's discussion on the Iraq letter was quite sad. What had the bishops to fear? Neither President Bush nor Saddam Hussein is waiting to see what the U.S. Catholic bishops say before making their decisions. But millions of Catholics and, one hopes, other Americans need to hear the moral argument, as well as the moral conclusion, the bishops' discussion would have provided in open debate. This bishops' conference is one of the few places in the Western world where war and peace are publicly discussed—with an accent on peace.

What finally came out of the closed episcopal session was a decision to have conference President Pilarczyk write the letter to Bush. Pilarczyk, writing in his own name as president, sent the letter November 15, informing the president that a war with Iraq "could well violate" Catholic moral teaching and saying that the "human, economic and other costs of war must be proportionate to the objective to be achieved by the use of weapons of war." Pilarczyk also asked Bush to ponder whether a war with Iraq would "leave the people of Kuwait, the Middle East and the world better or worse off?" The letter was based in traditional Catholic just-war thinking and continued to characterize most U.S. episcopal views—increasingly ineffective in the eyes of the *NCR*—straight through the war.

Like all other people, Americans have a light and dark side to their national character. We like to view ourselves as being an altruistic people, and stories abound that reveal that U.S. altruism. We can also covet our many blessings—and our appetite for material goods seems endless. With the Iraq invasion of Kuwait, Bush pushed his military response and worked to justify his Middle East policy. Listening to Bush, we discovered that the reasons we might have to go to war seemed to change by the hour. These changing rationales became the subject of comics' jokes and cartoonists' jibes. We were told we would have to go to war variously to protect the oil flow, to keep oil prices low, to protect jobs, to save the American way of life, to stop a madman from possessing nuclear and chemical weapons and to free Kuwait. Bush kept testing the waters, searching for that justification that would carry popular sentiment. It was very confusing to many people.

But after some weeks of experimentation, what seemed to sell best for Bush was a combination of the fear factor, plus jingoism, promises of a short, containable—in the administration's rhetoric—war, and a large dose of patriotic medicine. The fear factor played well. It melded fear from administration claims that Saddam Hussein was quickly gaining nuclear weapons, with fear of yet more unspeakable horrors being perpetrated by Iraq on Kuwait.

These arguments were working to wear down the largely Democratic opposition to Bush, an opposition that favored allowing sanctions more time to work. They also worked to counter the just-war "last resort" objection. Most bishops and other ethicists, from the right and left, may not have agreed on some matters pertaining to the Gulf War, but they did agree on one: More time was needed. All other peaceful channels had clearly not been tested. Peace feelers were aplenty and Iraq had been sending out signals through the Soviet Union and others that it might be willing to negotiate. But there would be no negotiations. Bush ensured that by not pursuing the diplomatic solution. War might have been avoided had Bush allowed Iraq the Middle East peace conference it had said it wanted in order to leave Kuwait (just as war might have been avoided had Bush gone the sanctions route). Such a conference could have been planned three to six months after an Iraqi withdrawal. But no, there could be no compromise. From the Catholic just-war point of view, this had seriously weakened Bush's "moral" hand and his handling of the debate. But as commander-in-chief and president he always had the upper hand on immediate action.

Just-war discussions, meanwhile, were breaking out every-where, on television, on college campuses, in parishes and on *NCR*'s pages. Bush was not to be left out. In a January 28 address, and possibly with an eye to taking on the critical Catholic bishops on their own terrain, the president appeared before a meeting of the National Religious Broadcasters, a conservative Protestant group, citing "just-war" theory with the presumed familiarity of a scholastic monk. But Bush's agenda was not so much the moral debate, at this point, as gathering support for "Desert Storm." In front of the broadcasters, he called the liberation of Kuwait a "just cause" and argued the "last resort" principle, saying he had initi-ated the war only after all diplomatic channels had been ex-hausted.

NCR media-watcher Jesuit Father Raymond Schroth was to pick this up in the February 22 issue:

. . . *Newsweek* (Jan. 28) reported the president's Christmas Camp David communing with God and Billy Graham's White House presence the night the war began.

Then the "just-war" terminology appeared in the State of the Union address, and we read the reiterated story that the Iraqis' murder of children had been the final straw that tipped his decision. Then the National Prayer Breakfast ap-pearance, and the declaration of Sunday, Feb. 3, as a na-tional day of prayer.

(Bush consultant) Roger Ailes, *Time*'s Hugh Sidey (Jan. 28) tells us, has successfully tutored the president on how to keep his wartime visage somber for the cameras. Bush also, according to *Newsweek* (Jan. 28), cut several references to the innocent victims of war from his televised war speech because, in practice, his voice cracked on the lines. Meanwhile, his aides have planted morality lines in all three newsweeklies. "I have resolved all moral questions in my mind. This is black and white, good versus evil," Sidey says Bush told his staff. An adviser told *U.S. News and*

World Report (Feb. 11), for an article on how Bush is modeling himself on Franklin D. Roosevelt and Abraham Lincoln, "the moral issue is the underpinning of the war for him."

In retrospect, it appears, Bush, aided by an all too uncritical media, was able to wipe out the last wavering doubts in the general populace. The day's "moral" debate in the public media—first framed by the U.S. bishops more than two months earlier, but then dropped when they retreated behind closed doors—was now co-opted by a resourceful president. With Augustine in his pocket, Bush had full freedom to pursue the war as he pleased. There would be no more serious threats from U.S. Catholic episcopal ranks.

An insightful Catholic News Service study published the following week and appearing in our February 15 issue, found, having studied nearly 100 U.S. Catholic bishops' statements, that before the bombing began, opposition to starting a war was nearly unanimous and that most episcopal moral assessments had focused on the just-war principle of last resort. The bishops felt it would be wrong to start a war, because all diplomatic channels to avoid bloodshed had not yet been explored. Once the war began, however, while the prelates continued to express "serious questions and reservations" about the war, they shifted their moral assessments to examine questions of proportionality and moral limitations on the conduct of war. In other words, almost no one was willing to condemn the war outright. Such a condemnation would mean risking confrontation with a determined president and an increasingly drum-beating U.S. public.

"To the extent there was a division among the bishops (before Jan. 16)," the article stated, "it was between those who said war would probably violate the just-war principles—a majority—and those who said it definitely would do so—a minority." This minority, the article went on, came mainly from the ranks of those bishops who were members of Pax Christi, the Catholic peace organization. At the time of the Gulf War, 91 belonged to Pax Christi U.S.A.

As January was ending and the bombing was well into its second week, *NCR* was also collecting episcopal statements. We attempted to reach every U.S. archbishop to get his thoughts on the war into the public record, even briefly excerpted. Published in our February 8 issue, the sentiments ran the gamut from those of Anchorage Archbishop Francis Hurley, who flatly stated he disagreed with Bush's view that the war was morally justified, to Cardinal Law, who stated that "even as we echo the prayer of Pope Paul VI, 'No more war; war never again,' with heavy hearts we realize that such a prayer is not fulfilled at the price of granting tyrants and aggressors an open field to achieve unjust ends."

The question being begged was: What would a serious analysis of the war look like if the just-war principles were invoked? I put it to *NCR* columnist Jesuit Father Robert Drinan, who answered in our Feb. 8 issue. Drinan's conclusion: this was an unjust war. One of the key passages in his assessment read:

> Of all the foregoing conditions required for a just war, perhaps the most important is the requirement of proportionality. In an excellent article on the morality of war in the Catholic Encyclopedia, Jesuit theologian Father Richard McCormick states firmly that "it is immoral directly to take innocent human life." McCormick goes on to state that, "if no other principles were violated by total warfare (they are), the immunity of noncombatants would be sufficient in itself to proscribe such warfare."

By now, the intensity of the debate was making me reflect in a manner that, later, produced this book. When, I wondered, had I stopped believing in the possibility of a just war? I decided it had most likely happened in Vietnam two decades earlier, although I had not realized it at the time. Perhaps it happened after I realized the extent to which just-war thinking had allowed church leaders to deviate from Jesus' teachings on love and forgiveness.

Or maybe I had scrapped the just-war theory as applicable to modern times and modern wars when I began to see that the theory was written more from the perspective of the perpetrators of war than from that of its victims. Maybe I had finally seen and reflected on the fact that the principles were more often used to justify rather than to resist war. Did my decision have something to do with the realization that the U.S. military—not unlike other militaries—lies, and distorts the truth during war, making informed wartime assessments virtually impossible? Had I, in the paper's editorial commentary over the looming war with Iraq, simply used the just-war principles one last time to free myself from their grip? Modern weapons, I realized, are so destructive that they are necessarily indiscriminate. (I dreamed once that the church condemned all wars after the first bomb was dropped from an airplane. What a wonderful dream. The bishops were arguing that the chances of miscalculation, were substantially greater at 30,000 feet with a bomb than at 10 feet with a bow and arrow. And as munitions would undoubtedly grow more powerful, no war fought with anything more lethal than bows and arrows could possibly be just. Of course, that was about the limit of weaponry when Augustine penned his just-war theory.)

Did Thomas Merton, Dorothy Day, Gordon Zahn, Phil and Dan Berrigan, Eileen Egan and Archbishop Hunthausen believe what their government told them in time of war? No. And neither do I. That's one of the things these pacifists and others taught me.

Looking back, I can honestly say that never did I believe the military and presidential claims about the accuracy of our bombings, highlighted by "smart bomb" videos. We were not being told then that smart bombs comprised only 7 percent of the total bombs being dropped. And we were not being told then that of the 88,500 tons dropped on Iraq and Kuwait, 70 percent were missing their targets. No, that information was withheld. Sitting in my Kansas City office in late January, thinking of the bombs dropping on Iraq, I decried the arrogance and immorality of my nation's actions in the Gulf. It was easy to see through the lies and self-justifications that inevitably followed. If truth is the first victim of war, how can religious leaders in a nation fighting that war expect to have the information needed to form sound judgments? Are there lessons here? While the bombers were finishing their second week, I wrote to make a point that I hoped would not be misunderstood. The comments appeared in my weekly column, "Inside NCR," in the February 8 issue:

> Personally, I think just-war discussions are helpful. From my view, however, they lead to a blanket condemnation of modern war. Once military ordnance began to be measured in tons, and soldiers began to lob artillery miles instead of meters and drop bombs from airplanes flying thousands of feet above the terrain, warfare became indiscriminate—and modern warfare immoral.
>
> The Franciscan nuns at St. Sebastian school in Milwaukee used to teach us, when in doubt about the morality of an action (usually fibbing or fighting on the playground then), ask if we could imagine Jesus doing it. Later, the Jesuits at Marquette High School echoed the idea (more sophisticatedly, of course), talking about the return to a Christocentric church and morality.
>
> I have tried to take these ideas seriously, not claiming here to have met with any long-term success. Nevertheless, to first justify this war, I would have to imagine Jesus in the cockpit of one of those B-52s we read about so much last week, and see his hand having just activated the releases to drop those scores of bombs on the Iraqi troops below. Were I able to envision this, were I to really believe Jesus could flip those switches, I would simply stop calling myself a follower of Christ.

A week later in a February 15 issue editorial, I stated it another way:

> The fact that 1,500 years and a thousand wars after Augustine—and eight years after the U.S. Catholic bishops'

peace letter—good portions of the nation are engaged in just-war debates is a sign of hope in otherwise dark times.

Maybe these analyses will one day move more leaders to conclude that modern warfare, in view of its destructive capabilities, is immoral. The U.S. bishops in their 1983 pastoral reminded us that modern warfare has brought humanity "to a moment of supreme crisis." This, it would seem, calls for categorically new thinking.

Might we dream of the human family, applying concepts such as proportionality, probability and right intention, would in the light of current circumstances finally reject war? Might we further dream it would also one day take seriously those ancient yet totally relevant Judeo-Christian admonitions our faiths have kindled in our souls, the commandments "Thou shall not kill" and "Love thy enemies as thyself." What a world that would be!

Just imagine.

7

"If You Want Peace, Work for Justice"

"Ours is a just cause," President Bush said, exalting the U.S. war effort in the Persian Gulf. By "just" he meant proper or morally correct. It is ironic, when you think of it, that he should use the word. "Just" is derived from the same Latin root, *justus*, as the word "justice," meaning fair, impartial or equitable. To be moral and to support justice are two concepts linked by more than the language we use. When a U.S. president can refer to the U.S. war against Iraq as "just," the irony turns to tragedy. The fact is that U.S. policies toward the Middle East have never stressed justice. President Jimmy Carter, for the most part, was an exception. The Camp David accords, for which he was largely responsible, were a magnificent exception. Sadly, U.S. foreign policy has never been aimed at the building of a fairer or more equitable order in the Middle East. To the contrary, U.S. policies there reveal a pattern in which U.S. officials have consistently taken sides with the rich and powerful, often at the expense of the poor. U.S. policies have often been aimed at advancing the interests of *corporate* America with disregard for furthering the interests of *civil* America. In the Middle East, oil has been king. And the American government wants to maintain control of the court.

During the Gulf War, our principal allies were the two richest families of the Middle East (and probably the world), the Saud family of Saudi Arabia and the al-Sabah family of Kuwait, feudal monarchs and owners of multibillion-dollar oil companies. Meanwhile, nine out of ten Arabs, or more than 90 percent of the region's 150 million Arabs, live in poverty. The United States has sent what it calls aid in the form of modern weapons, in quantitites far exceeding that needed for self-defense. This "aid" has been good for U.S. business; it has helped the U.S. balance of trade. But the poor cannot eat metal.

While no U.S. policy, however redirected, however well-intended, will quickly alter the stark reality of Middle East poverty, any U.S. policy that either ignores that poverty or adds to the injustice of the areas' conditions is neither moral nor in the long-term self-interest of the United States.

History, too, shows that while a temporary "order" can be imposed at the point of a gun barrel, it cannot be sustained. And one day its victims will turn on their oppressors. So the cycle of violence is renewed. How, we must ask, do we break this seemingly endless cycle? It is not a lack of vision that holds the world back. It is a lack of will. The vision is already widely shared, but it involves education, not more weapons. It is a vision that sadly threatens those who cling to their power and cling to the past. Either history will one day overtake them, or life as we know it on planet Earth will end.

In the late 20th century, the human family has become aware for the first time of the many ways its life patterns are woven into and are part of the fabric of larger planetary life systems. Many of us now understand how the coveting and misuse of resources by any region or people disturbs the larger symbiotic web. Meanwhile, as the human family begins to see itself as integral to the whole, it is also becoming more aware of the responsibilities it owes to other family members. It is all part of the same sacred vision, from the smallest measurable particle to the outermost reaches of the universe. Yet, only now are we beginning to understand that the poets, mystics, theologians, physical and social scientists are playing the same orchestral composition.

Our governmental leaders and those who run the armies that support them have not yet seriously considered this message that is all too obvious to others. In the closing years of the 20th century, we are very close to major breakthroughs in accepting the concept of total creational unity, yet, knowing this, we feel so very far away. When we say war is obsolete, we mean it; when we say war must be relegated to history, we mean it. Knowing what we know, whether as Christians or as modern world citizens, increases our responsibility to continue to pursue the journey in the face of apparent defeat.

Our churches *have begun* to shift slightly in recognizing the meaning of the sacred in a manner that previously only a few of the saints—St. Francis leaps out as an obvious candidate—hinted at or proclaimed in years past. Part of my new understanding is intertwined with lessons I learned in the process of familiarizing myself with a century of what is loosely called the Catholic church's social teachings. These are rooted in the 1891 letter, or encyclical, *Rerum Novarum*, written by Pope Leo XIII. The most recent, related letter is Pope John Paul II's *Sollicitudo Rei Socialis* (1987). Each of these teachings, and those in between, stresses the sacred vision of which I write. Here is the point: Catholic social teaching has helped to lay a foundation that indicates the range of our responsibilities within an entire mystical universe, the dimensions of which only now, with the help of modern science, are we beginning to imagine. These social writings have already pointed out pathways of understanding essential for the continued development of life on the planet. Most importantly, these documents reiterate that human beings, as children of the Creator, have essential rights that include the rights to life, to adequate food, shelter and fruitful labor. These documents have shared their writers' passion for justice, for a vision of a world order founded in that justice, founded in an equitable sharing of the world resources. Each document has also emphasized that those blessed with abundance are required to share with those not so blessed. All these visions can be traced to Christian Gospel teachings, to the words and acts of Jesus Christ.

Pope Paul VI gave us the phrase, and command, "If you want peace, work for justice." The comment is so familiar among many Catholics that it appears frequently on bumper stickers. All this attests to a simple fact: many Christians view the world differently from most other people. Their Christian vision of the future is founded in the belief that faith calls them to work for a new world order—but not just any new order. No, their faith calls them to work for a new world order founded in justice, and, where justice is insufficient to meet the problems, in mercy. It calls them to work for life, for lasting peace, and, where peace is merely the absence of war, to work for harmony based on active reconciliation. It calls them to work to form a relationship between people and the natural order, and, where peaceful coexistence alone is insufficient, to promote it through the blending of science and myth, belief and the arts.

In a general way I offer this fact—that we as Christians are expected to view the world differently—as one explanation of why I viewed the U.S.-led war against Iraq as I did. It also affected my decision to send a member of the *NCR* staff to Canberra, Australia, in February where the World Council of Churches (WCC) was to have its seventh general assembly. In recent years, the WCC has been out in front of most other church leaders, including many in the Catholic church, in efforts to integrate Christian peace and justice themes into concerns for the environment. A year earlier, for example, the WCC held a major conference in Seoul, Korea, titled "Justice, Peace and the Integrity of Creation." Many of those Christians have been coming to profoundly new understandings of ecological relationships and the inevitability of having to find ways to implement these in order to foster peace and justice goals. These were our thoughts as we prepared for *NCR* coverage of the Australian WCC meeting. However, all that was before Saddam Hussein invaded Kuwait. In Canberra, as it turned out, the environment had to take a backseat to war and its victims' sufferings in

Canberra. There is something else to be said of this particular WCC gathering as it turned its focus on the U.S. share of the responsibility for turning the Iraq invasion of Kuwait into a bloody conflict. The WCC gathering gave us a rare opportunity to see ourselves—and our nation's policies in the Persian Gulf—as others were seeing us. As my father used to say: That ability constitutes the first step to wisdom.

It turned out to be fortuitous that we sent national news editor Pat Windsor to Canberra. We learned more than we expected—and some of it came with no little pain. We placed Windsor's first file from Canberra on the front page of our February 22 issue under the headline: "World Council of Churches finds agenda occupied by Persian Gulf War issues." These excerpts reveal the deep anguish felt and expressed at the gathering. Although a half a world away and lacking any measurable secular power, conference attendees addressed the war issues with all the spiritual might they could muster. They were—as were many of us in the United States at the time—feeling the loneliness of powerlessness to influence, even marginally, the course of world events. But while many Americans were at the time sharing with me expressions of isolation from the wider, war-supporting public, at least I could take comfort in knowing that this American minority was, in fact, connected in spirit to a significant and influential worldwide network, the second-largest Christian worldwide network, second only to the Roman Catholic Church. Perhaps as much as any church body in recent years, the World Council of Churches has become a voice for the marginalized of the earth. It has taken its share of risks, has funded programs unpopular with Western governments and others rooted to the status quo in former Western colonies and has stood up to a goodly number of dictators and tyrants. The WCC has earned the credentials to speak on behalf of the Third World poor. What Windsor heard in Canberra, then, were often voices representing especially vulnerable people. The Canberra voices spoke on behalf of victims of war, almost from the bomb craters of Iraq:

The Iraqi bishop's peace plea to the World Council of Churches' Seventh Assembly Feb. 12 was passionate, and it was not about oil but about children.

"When I left Baghdad," said Assyrian Bishop Sliwa Gewargis, "there were thousands of children's eyes looking at me saying, 'Please tell the World Council of Churches that we prefer the smell of roses to the smell of oil; we like to listen to choirs . . . and we do not like to hear the thunder of bombs.'

"I am anxious and afraid. Please, let me take hope back to these children . . . if I can find them alive in Baghdad." Gewargis' plea came as WCC delegates debated how to respond to the Gulf crisis, a topic uppermost in the minds of most of about 3,500 participants during the early days of their Feb. 7-20 assembly, at times overshadowing the assembly's theme, "Come Holy Spirit, Renew the Whole Creation." As the first week of the assembly came to a close, differences emerged between those calling for an immediate, unconditional cease-fire—including the WCC's general secretary, several Third World delegates and the U.S. delegation—and others, led by the Church of England, advocating a cease-fire only if linked to an Iraqi pullout of Kuwait. . . .

In an opening address that would set the tone for the assembly, Sir Paul Reeves, Anglican representative to the United Nations in New York and former governor general of New Zealand, said the Gulf War is "neither holy nor just." Several subsequent speakers picked up on the theme, categorically rejecting Iraq's claims of "holy war" and the West's claims of "just war," in a move seen as clear rejection of traditional just-war teaching."

These were also among the Third World pleas Windsor recorded:

- Oriental Orthodox Archbishop Aram Keshishian (of Armenia): The war is a "Third World war" with "far-reaching, destructive, global implications."

- Father Tissa Balasuriya, Sri Lankan: "This is 1492 all over again." Only this time, he said, the United States is seeking to dominate the Middle East.

- Jean Zaru, Palestinian: ". . . Are you setting the Palestinians an example that we should solve our problems by force?"

- Emilio Castro, Uruguayan, WCC general secretary: "As churches of Jesus Christ, it is our (mandate) to call for a cease-fire."

On its final day, February 20, the assembly issued an emphatic plea to the warring parties: "Cease the bombing! Still the missiles! Stop the fighting! Restrain your armies! Negotiate! Trust in the promise of peace!"

The WCC statement decried the "widening effects" of the war on Middle East tensions, further asserting that the conflict was diverting the world's attention from other "massive human tragedies."

Partly as a result of talking with Windsor by phone and reading her dispatches midway through the 43-day Persian Gulf War, I began to realize how different this war was being perceived outside the United States. *NCR* columnist Rosemary Radford Ruether, in India at the time, was picking up the same information. Later, she wrote a column (*NCR*, March 1) quoting an editorial writer in the New Delhi *Hindustan Times*. Wrote Ruether: "(He) summed up the general view of Indians in these words: 'The war is certainly not for saving democracy or a fight against dictatorship. All this is nonsense. They have no such interest. There is no such interest. Their interest is in oil. As (Henry) Kissinger put it very picturesquely: 'to have assured supplies and at an acceptable price.' Now, this is the real game.'"

By then, Bush had successfully depicted the war solely as a self-less effort aimed at freeing the Kuwaiti people from a ruthless occupying army. But among other people—as Windsor, Ruether and others overseas I kept speaking to could attest—especially those in poorer nations, the war was being viewed as one waged by the rich against the poor. It was being viewed as a war by the haves of the world against the have-nots, by those who controlled the world's wealth against those who did not.

In the post-Cold War era, with the East-West battle between capitalism and communism seemingly fading into history, this war was of a new breed. It was being seen in foreign lands as the first North-South war. One day in my office in late January 1991, I had heard three people on three different continents independently refer to the war as a North-South conflict, a battle over resources between the rich and the poor that the rich intend to win. That such perceptions existed, apart from any examination of the veracity of the charge, should be enough to send shudders down the spines of all Americans. I pondered the implications of these North-South perceptions again and again in the weeks that followed and, as I did, I became increasingly disturbed. I began to ask myself if all of us—even the knowledgeable critics—were underestimating the propaganda strength of our government to make us think what it wanted us to. I remember asking myself, "Could this be what it was like to be a German during World War II?" Not so much that we were Germans in the Persian Gulf. But were we as cut off from the ability to see ourselves as the outside world saw us as the Germans were during World War II? Inside Germany, inside that propaganda machine, Germans got up, went to work, loved their children, ate food—and supported the war. Most believed it to be just. I asked myself: Could it be that inside the United States—blanketed in U.S. war hysteria and dependent on a press so seemingly submissive and committed to the establishment view that it does not even need to be government-controlled— Americans were so cut off from the rest of the world that we were blind to reality? Of course we were. As we are blind to so many other realities clearly visible when we take a few steps back and look at ourselves. Plenty of evidence indicates that the Gulf War was about oil. Otherwise, why attack Iraq and not, say, Turkey, Syria, Indonesia or any number of other aggressor nations to which we turn a blind eye? Some Americans readily admit that the war, in fact, was about oil. They say without hesitation that the war was about "protecting U.S. economic interests in the Middle East," about keeping the price of oil low. And they applaud it. But what does this say to the rest of the world, which pays four times the price for comparable oil, which sees us use more than twice the amount of energy as the same number of people in Europe?

The most penetrating questions being asked and answered at the WCC gathering in Canberra were frequently from people who saw Middle East events primarily through the eyes of the poor. As I read the dispatches from Canberra, the poor preeminent in the coverage, I was regularly reminded of Penny Lernoux, *NCR*'s Latin American affairs writer from the mid-1970s until her death, in October 1989. Lernoux's writings changed the way a vibrant segment of an entire generation looks at Latin America. For most Americans, it is almost impossible to envision their nation as an oppressive power. But not so for those who first learned of what the United States was doing in Latin American through Lernoux's articles and books, including her classic *Cry of the Poor* (1980). Lernoux brought home to North America the significance in both Latin American and North American terms the radical changes the Catholic church in Latin America was undergoing in the wake of the Vatican Council as it took up its now famous "preferential option for the poor." She not only described the intentions of this church, she brought to the North the personalities of the new breed of Latin American theologians practicing a new theology, "liberation theology." She wrote about the persecution these theologians endured sometimes from within their own churches but more often from the military dictators who ruthlessly ran their nations with U.S. support. Lernoux wrote about this new church's living saints and counted its young martyrs, men and women, prominent and not, who died for speaking out on behalf of the poor, for preaching the Gospels. "The Word will set you free." In Latin America, she wrote, it all too often also led to death.

During the Gulf War, Lernoux would unexpectedly intrude on my thoughts as I grappled with trying to present to the reader the underside of what was happening: looking at this war from the bottom up, instead of from the top down, as the general media was presenting it. When I was feeling bewildered about trying to get across a vision, a view, a perspective, an argument that begins with, "Wait, things aren't as they appear to be," I would remember Lernoux. For I was feeling the powerlessness of which she had so often written.

She readily admitted that at first she merely reported what she was hearing the poor say to her. But before long, she realized, they were becoming a part of her. She picked up their faith and carried their strength, and through her they became our brothers and sisters to the South. What Lernoux finally accomplished was to make the economic and political as well as spiritual connections between the South and the North. She showed us the North-South divide in people terms and discussed that divide from the Catholic Christian perspective and mandate:

> I believe that those who seek a new path, whether in the church or secular society, should not expect roses but must be prepared to endure the prophet's life in the desert. Yet, as the (Brazilian) archbishop (Helder Camara) notes, "the desert also blooms"—as we have seen in Latin America. . . . Meanwhile, those of us committed to the church of Medellin and to Vatican II must continue the struggle. Sometimes it is hard, as I know from my reporting on the church in Latin America, but I also believe it is the only way to remain steadfast to Christ's vision.

Vintage Lernoux.

And what I have attempted here is to provide yet another element to our Persian Gulf coverage, how Lernoux's faith, vision, spirit and energy played a large role in keeping us on course. Perhaps at the newspaper many of us have internalized Lernoux. We have certainly tried to.

Looking out at the world, seeking peace with justice in mind, forced us throughout the war to ask questions that most other people simply were not asking.

What did the Iraq conflict demand of us as U.S. citizens, as Christians and as members of a universal church? There are times when our national and universal identities come into conflict. When they do, we must give precedence to our *universal* identities. Seeing life through the eyes of a universal church necessitates incorporating the feelings and sufferings of the poor, whether in the Middle East or Latin America or Africa or Asia firmly into the equation. Justice questions raise their demanding heads to disturb us. To live universally is to be *one*. It means to celebrate *communion*. It means to finally accept the mystery of being the Body of Christ, as Paul tells us we are. And one body does not go to war with itself. It works to protect itself and grow. We are not there yet, but we know the way and we are moving down the path. *That* is a just cause.

8

Faith and Resistance

It seemed as incongruous as anything I might have imagined in the Middle East at the time—and as dangerous, too. The plans called for an international group of activists to set up camp between the opposing armies as a peace buffer. It was late December and as Western and Arab armies made their final preparations for battle, the Gulf Peace Team was getting set to move toward the Iraqi-Saudi border at the center of an imaginary triangle connecting the Middle East capitals of Baghdad, Riyadh and Amman. There were more than a hundred on the team and they were entering the region through Iraq. They carried simple supplies and began to live in tents. They pledged to remain there, in the desert, as peace symbols with the outside hope their presence might somehow thwart the outbreak of war. They were to be nonaligned, they said, an international peacekeeping group representing those many millions pleading for a nonviolent, negotiated solution to the region's problems. When we learned of the team's plans in December, we knew we wanted to follow their activities—but how? At least a score of Americans were joining the team. Further, we figured, their presence on the border would likely be ignored by much of the rest of the press.

When you think of it, it really was an interesting story. There would be hundreds of thousands of men and women from around the world in uniform present and set for battle. Wouldn't the hundred coming to protest that battle also be newsworthy? We thought so. Managing editor Dawn Gibeau made contact with a

New York writer, Jim O'Grady, who was already in touch with the group. By phone from New York in the weeks that followed, he was able to gather information on the group's activities. For more than a month, we ran O'Grady's reports, accounts that quickly captured our readers' interest and imagination. After the first report, we began receiving phone calls from anxious people wanting to know if the group was safe or how it was doing. Some people called almost daily seeking information. We told them whatever we knew, which sometimes wasn't much.

Dispatches were irregular. Communications were spotty, especially once the bombing began. The following piece is excerpted from O'Grady's January 25 dispatch. It gives the flavor of his reports and underscores the contradiction the team represented to many during those weeks in the battle zone:

> At a stopover during the trip to the Middle East, Anthony Lawrence sat in a Kennedy Airport lounge chair and turned in his hands a wallet-sized photo of his 22-year-old son, Charles. Fear for his son's life, Lawrence said, moved him to volunteer to join the Gulf Peace Camp, a temporary settlement on the Iraq and Saudi border that intended by its peaceful presence to slow the region's plunge toward war. Yet, even as Anthony Lawrence spoke on a gloomy evening Jan. 12, his son Charles sat on highest alert with his U.S. Army helicopter squadron in the Saudi Arabian desert.

> So as the hours separating the world from war evaporated, father and son apparently converged on the same speck of desert wasteland, and the man staring at the photograph may soon have to endure the poignant absurdity of being overrun and possibly killed, by military forces that include his son. . . .

> Anthony Lawrence traveled as part of a 14-person second wave of American citizens to the Gulf Peace Camp, which now numbers 120 people from 21 countries, according to organizers. The camp—a concrete-covered expanse

about the size of three football fields, surrounded by wire mesh and dotted with tents—is located at Judayyidat-'Ar'-Ar, a traditional desert way station for Mecca-bound pilgrims.

Once word of the team's mission was out, organizers began to be deluged with support letters. One in particular gave them special comfort, they said. It came from Mother Teresa of Calcutta, who wrote: ". . . As much as I would have loved to be with you, I am not able, but you have our prayers and sacrifices. . . . Do not be afraid—remember works of love are works of peace."

The team stayed on. It remained well after the United States and its allies began to bomb Iraq. It ignored many Iraqi warnings. Team members claimed that Iraqi officials, having earlier given them permission to set up the camp, were now feeling a personal responsibility for the team's safety. Meanwhile, conditions were deteriorating. Pressure to shut down the camp grew. Finally, after the peace camp ignored Iraqi requests to leave, soldiers forced the peace activists out January 27, more than a month after they originally pitched their tents. One Gulf Peace Team organizer based in London, hearing of their eviction, told *NCR*: "They've been a magnificent counterblast of sanity and reason amid an area of madness; they've served as a tangible focus for people around the world who want peace in the Middle East. We're very proud of them." The Gulf Peace Team might end up no more than a footnote in history, but it represented something significant—an internationally coordinated act of resistance to war in the midst of a war. And it is the type of footnote *NCR*'s editors believe tell as much about history as the main text. I wondered if, years from now, the Peace Team might even be viewed as the larger story. The Gulf War, one might argue, was one of the 35 or so wars occurring around the world in early 1991, albeit, by far, the most prominent. But the international peace team, all volunteers and sharing a common vision, came to a spot in the midst of war to exclaim "No!" They were witnessing to Pope Paul VI's words at the United Nations: "No more war; war never again!"

I also wondered who were the people in all those different nations responsible for planting the seeds of those peace visions. And how did their convictions grow so firm that they were willing to risk their lives for what they believed? Over the years, interviewing peace activists, I have often asked people who the single biggest influence in their lives was. It is interesting to see who had influenced this or that person. Names connect continents and move back through the generations. Many of today's activists trace their convictions to people active in the 1960s, the Berrigans, Dorothy Day, Dr. Martin Luther King, Jr., for example. Occasionally, the name of a bishop might arise, but it was not until the early 1980s that most U.S. Catholics could line up the entire conference of U.S. Catholic bishops as significant—once the U.S. bishops themselves acted by publishing their 1983 peace pastoral.

It is important to note that the entire name of that episcopal letter was "The Challenge of Peace: God's Promise and Our Response." What was to be "our response"? Many, indeed, responded to the bishops. Some began to teach peace in the classrooms. Some took the pastoral into the local parishes and insisted they become familiar with its contents. Many purposefully took on simpler lifestyles. Many protested and deplored violence. Some went further, risking their jobs, reputations and even their lives. Some blocked military convoys, others blocked trains carrying nuclear weapons. Many began military tax protests. Some fasted for peace, days and weeks at a time. Others planned prayer vigils, wrote peace liturgies or composed new prayers. Some began working in local interfaith peace networks. Others joined and contributed to peace organizations such as Pax Christi U.S.A. Some began doing civil disobedience. They jumped fences at nuclear missile sites and hung peace banners, threw blood on U.S. military buildings and blocked military training centers. Others protested ROTC on Catholic campuses. Some went to faith and resistance retreats, mapped nuclear weapons sites, went to prison. For these acts, some received sentences of up to 10 or more years. For such nonviolent crimes they were viewed by many inside and outside the

United States as political prisoners. At no time had the nation seen acts of resistance quite like these. They were of a new breed, born of a new awareness and commitment to peace values.

Looking back, it seems many of these peace protests during the 1980s stemmed from a radical awakening of conscience touched off by what many viewed as a growing and very dangerous militarism in America. At *NCR*, we measured this militarism in stories we did each year on the budgets being proposed by the Reagan White House. More for Trident submarines, less for hot lunches. More for MX missiles, less for inner-city health care. More for Star Wars research, less for federal aid for education. Let no one argue it was not happening. It could be measured annually and was happening even though the nation lacked the money to pay for increased military spending.

In the 1980s the nation spent virtually all it wanted for new weapons. Taxes, especially for the rich, were cut so they could spend their money to, it was said, "stimulate the economy." But the super-rich, instead of investing, began to buy out other corporations. Leveraged buyouts and the cannibalization of corporations became the rage. Forget the jobs lost. The super-rich were free to act as they wished. Wealth became increasingly concentrated among the very rich. Between 1981 and 1988, the net worth of the Forbes 400 richest Americans tripled. When the decade began, the nation had only a handful of billionaires. When it ended, it had more than 50 billionaires and 1,200 centimillionaires, 100,000 decamillionaires and 1.5 million millionaires. To this day, the American public has not yet realized just how much money was sucked by the super-rich from the pockets of the middle class and the poor during the runaway 1980s.

Deficits, meanwhile, grew and grew. In 1980, the United States, the largest creditor nation, had a trade surplus of $166 billion; by August 1987, it had become the largest debtor nation, with an indebtedness to foreigners of $340 billion. Borrow and spend for new weapons was the rule. The defense buildup was to be paid for by generations not yet born when Reagan was president.

And the poor got poorer. The nation tottered on bankruptcy. Simultaneously, the 1980s were also characterized by a kind of military madness. The nation built weapons of mass destruction it could never use—and still survive. This militarism was fueled by those whose interest it was to inflate the Soviet threat to gargantuan proportions. First create and then inflate a climate of fear; next, propose the military response. Tried and true. Echoes of Saddam Hussein. There was never anything rational about arming our nation with 25,000 nuclear weapons. Yet, even after the Soviet Union had virtually collapsed in the early 1990s, little evidence could be found that U.S. policymakers were ready or willing to change their course or fundamental presuppositions. If there were no Soviet threat, then, perhaps, the Pentagon could establish itself as the new global police force, paid for, in part, by the other rich nations of the world.

To say no to madness and immorality, sometimes all one can do is stand as a public witness. Many did. That's essentially what the Gulf Peace Team was doing on the Iraq-Saudi border. During the 1980s, we covered many peace witnesses. I would argue that they were among the most important stories of the decade. Far into the future, people will, I believe, see the 1980s as the decade in which many Americans, among them many U.S. Christians, finally began to say no to U.S. militarism, moving from simple protest to active resistance. Conscience compelled them to do so.

If, in the 1970s, many Christians found bold examples of faith commitment among the marginalized justice-seeking poor of Latin America, in the 1980s they could find similarly bold examples in their own ranks among the peace-seekers. More than anything else, what appeared to connect the two movements and two continents was the common conviction that their faith demanded active responses to conditions around them that they found to be intolerable. Both decades saw Christians willingly accept the risks involved in making responses. And as word of these examples spread, they spawned new activism. The Gulf War may well end up being a catalyst to help shape the 1990s—and not quite in the fashion the Bush White House had expected.

During the 1980s, two opposing visions of America were visible and gaining momentum. They were on a collision course as they competed for the soul of the nation. While the Pentagon had virtually all the money it wanted (and new prominence at the close of the Iraq war), the vision out of which it had been growing—East-West confrontation—appeared to be fading into history. Is it too cynical to suggest that the military and its industrial coalition, the weapons and systems-making corporations, were searching for new justifications to maintain its prominence? Peace activists, meanwhile, were forging new and creative bonds with environmentalists and together were forming a powerful vision of a truly new world order, an order steeped in ecological understanding and inspired by a radical new awareness of the sacredness of creation. This vision was gaining momentum around the world, and as we entered the 1990s—despite the horror of Iraq—this developing partnership had the appearance of being the single most important vision capable of guiding the planet into the 21st century.

How reassuring it is to be able to reach back into recent memory—or in the case of a newspaper, into recent clips—to recall who these people were who stood up to U.S. militarism in the 1980s. We wrote about many, some prominent, others not. None was insignificant. Each in some small way changed the shape and course of the peace movement and churches, if not history itself. Recall and consider some of these names:

- Pope John Paul II, at Hiroshima, February 25, 1981: "Let us pledge ourselves to peace through justice. Let us take a solemn decision, now, that war will never be tolerated or sought as a means of resolving differences; let us promise our fellow human beings that we will work untiringly for disarmament and the banishing of all nuclear weapons."

- James R. Sauder, who on Oct. 7, 1981, wearing a black, pin-striped suit, holding a crucifix in one hand, climbed over a security fence at a Titan II missile site near Conway, Ark., where for a half-hour before being arrested, he performed what he called religious rituals aimed at protesting the nuclear arms race.

  "I have a renewed sense of hope," he later wrote in *NCR*. "If I, one fairly ordinary person, can stand up in a forthright manner, can speak the truth to an unbelieving world and then take the flack for it, imprisonment, trial, probation, continuing hassles, then others can, too."

- Carol Fennelly, Mary Ellen Hombs and Mitch Snyder, who in March and April 1982 fasted for 64 days before the U.S. Navy agreed to change the name of a nuclear attack submarine from the "USS Corpus Christi" to the "USS City of Corpus Christi." An *NCR* editorial stated at the time: "To Christians who believe Jesus Christ to be the Son of God and the Prince of Peace, the name was an obscene act."

- Sidney Lens, author of more than 20 books and a 1983 three-part *NCR* series, "The Militarization of a Democracy," which began: "Though we still have one president and one Congress in the United States, we now have, in effect, two governments. One government remains open, moderately democratic; the other persists in the shadows, secret and authoritarian." His 1977 book, *Day before Doomsday*, awakened me to the nuclear threat.

- Benedictine Sister Barbara McCracken, who taught the U.S. bishops peace pastoral and spent endless hours gathering and reviewing peace literature to edit and produce a half-dozen *NCR* Teaching Peace and Justice guides for educators.

• Juli Loesch, founder of Pro-lifers for Survival, the antinuclear and antiabortion organization that worked to knit a complete sacred-life fabric.

• James and Shelley Douglass, founders of Ground Zero for Nonviolent Action, who purchased a home near the Bangor Submarine Base in the state of Washington to track the White Trains carrying nuclear weapons across America. They also helped awaken Seattle Archbishop Raymond Hunthausen to the nuclear threat. James Douglass showed up at the White House in the middle of the Gulf War and began a fast for peace.

• The Plowshares, scores of risk-taking, antinuclear activists who protested at nuclear missile sites and went to prison for their beliefs. "Peacemaking is not an optional commitment. It is required by faith," four Plowshares said in a statement they issued, quoting from the U.S. bishops' peace pastoral. The four, arrested November 12, 1984, included Oblate Fathers Paul and Carl Kabat, Larry Cloud-Morgan and Helen Woodson.

• The Catholic Workers who continued the movement's traditions of hospitality to the poor and nonviolence as a way of life.

• Sam Day, editor, Nukewatch activist. The organization spent many months mapping the precise locations of U.S. strategic weapon sites, raising local and national consciousness.

• Jim Wallis and the Sojourners community, whose writings and peace actions have been an inspiration for many.

• Faith and Resistance retreats organizers and participants who combined Gospel reflections with personal lifestyle reassessments. For many, these retreats ended in acts of civil disobedience.

- Sister of Notre Dame Mary Evelyn Jegen, former Pax Christi U.S.A. national coordinator and Benedictine Sister Mary Lou Kownacki, current Pax Christi national coordinator. They helped chart the organization through a decade of growth.

These are a few of the many whose vision and faith were influencing the peace movement in the 1980s. Most of their work continues. For example, from Christmas through the beginning of the Iraq war, Jegen kept a vigil in front of the White House. She carried a sign one day that said, "The most beautiful victory will be the war we never fight." She was not alone. On January 15 and 16, the day the bombs began to drop, 1,200 protesters were arrested in the streets of 13 U.S. cities.

Detroit Auxiliary Bishop Thomas Gumbleton has been another source of inspiration to many. The month before the United States began bombing Iraq, he visited Baghdad, spending time in the home of an Iraqi Christian family. There are 500,000 Chaldean Christians among Baghdad's four million population.

"Here were people struggling to live a normal life. They were dreading the thought of their teens going off to war. We sat and talked in their house in Baghdad," he told NCR after the visit. "When the bombs are falling, a house like this is probably going to be blown up and these people killed.

"A city with this huge concentration of people—it just made me realize how terrible war would be."

What keeps a Gumbleton going, even during the Gulf War when there seemed so little reason for encouragement? I have often wondered from where the energy comes.

Over the years as NCR editor, I have watched these peacemakers and interviewed many of them. It appears to come down to this: Their work and beliefs are one. So they simply cannot stop. To do so would be to abandon their beliefs, to be people they are not. Jesuit Father Dan Berrigan, asked once what kept him going, responded: "I resist because I cannot not resist." Peace activists instinctively understand what Berrigan meant. We know what he was thinking and doing during the Gulf War. The same holds true for those mentioned above and the tens of thousands not mentioned.

Knowing this should reassure us. It should help us know that we were not really isolated in our anguish during the war, even when it appeared we were.

It should help us accept that we were not "crazy" when we found ourselves the only persons in our offices or families or among friends who deeply opposed what the United States was doing in the Middle East. It may help to remember, too, that very late in Christ's life, during his passion and leading up to his death, he felt alone, even abandoned.

But he was not. Nor were we. Our beliefs in the lasting power of love, forgiveness, compassion and nonviolence are well placed. And they are not meant as personal pieties, but rather as radical commitments to all creation, as prayerful acts of eternal gratitude to our Creator.

Remember, after the hysteria dies, there will be time for more quiet reflection. The drumbeats of war cannot be sustained. Watch. The peacemakers' ranks will continue to grow.

9

War: "On Schedule"

It was nearing mid-February. The war, Bush told us, was "on schedule." Though hardly intended, his words smacked of arrogance. They came across as cold and detached. The intended message was that this president was a masterful planner who could deliver according to some unstated and secret master plan. But I felt his remarks had a heartless quality, as if he had entirely lost touch with the real human consequences of this war, as if all the deaths occurring in Iraq had been pre-planned, all part of the master's calculation.

Bush master-minded the momentum which eventually carried many nations to war. He was the driver. He knew the course. He was in control. Not to worry. The trip would cause no undue hardship. That was key. We did not want hardship. We did not want additional taxes. We did not want our sons or daughters dead. Perhaps a few deaths were tolerable. But not many. That was the bargain. And it had to be over soon. We had to get on with other things. As for Iraq, his plans presumably included the destruction of a greater part of the nation and the killing of 100,000 or more. Was the turmoil of a post-war-ravaged Iraq also scheduled?

I fought my growing anger when I thought of Bush's actions. He must know. He must know what happens in war, I thought. What leads a person to such detached heights? I never satisfactorily found the answers I searched for. It has been difficult to quell the anger.

The bombings had continued for nearly a month. The Pentagon had long since declared "air supremacy"—meaning allied aircraft could bomb virtually uncontested anywhere in Iraq. Night and day the bombs fell. Iraq was virtually defenseless. Its leaders were being brought to their knees, but at an enormous price to the people of Iraq. The discussion going on among U.S. military pundits at the time was how long to continue these "softening up" exercises. The focus was still on the coming ground war. The Iraqi troops in and around Kuwait were being hit hardest of all. The reason for the bombings—logical within the context of the war— was that the more Iraqis the allies could kill first, the fewer allied casualties there would be later.

Supply lines, we were told, had become key targets. Bombs were being dropped around the clock on roads and bridges. Again and again, we watched laser-guided "smart bombs" falling toward their targets. Precision bombing, these, or so we were led to believe. We became voyeurs of violence, gratified by a display of U.S. military supremacy. Seldom, if ever, in military history had such overwhelming superiority been achieved so quickly. Iraq was clearly a wounded animal. And we were safe to kick it at will. Perhaps the last time the United States was so clearly in a league by itself was when it dropped nuclear bombs on Hiroshima and Nagasaki, in August 1944. Only this time we got to bask in our military might almost daily as Pentagon briefers shared with us the "smart bomb" videos it chose to make their point. U.S. technology at work! A young boy, my nephew, 13, tells his mother he wants to grow up to be an Air Force pilot. Another type of war victim. But we were all fascinated. We watched the bombs fall, fastening our attention, as requested by the briefers, to the center of the target. Seconds passed . . . and puff. We never heard the explosions. The fact that we never heard the explosions is at the core of the next chapter, a chapter on the violence that war is.

The explosions looked like small firecrackers, but trucks and houses—and presumably people—would disappear. On one occasion as we waited for a bomb to hit a targeted bridge, a small vehicle passed through the cross hairs of the cockpit video screen, escaping the blast by seconds. Reviewing one day's work, a grinning General Norman Schwarzkopf, who later told us his favorite prayer is St. Francis' Prayer of Peace, chuckled and said that truck driver was the "the luckiest man" in Iraq. How many of us chuckled with him? It was so dehumanizing. We, too, were being targeted by the military. We, too, were becoming victims of those bombs. Someday, I hoped then, watching that bomb drop, we would come to understand.

The Iraqi government initially tried to hide the bomb damage, seemingly because admitting it would confirm its inability to defend itself and its people. But faced with the growing devastation, Saddam Hussein decided that showing this would be in his interest. Iraqi officials began to escort foreign broadcasters, including CNN's Peter Arnett, to civilian casualties, with encouragement to beam them out to the world. This was the beginning of the end of the war, the beginning of the end of the bombing.

To set this final scene, we need to step back one last time. We have reached the chronological point in the Gulf War narrative at which the ground war is less than two weeks away. We are within hours of awakening to learn that two U.S. "smart bombs" had blasted through the top of an underground bomb shelter in downtown Baghdad, killing hundreds of Iraqi civilians.

As we review how far we have come in this narrative, we see we have examined:

- The Bush administration and its motives,
- The home front and the popular hysteria,
- The media and its frustrations,
- And the moral leadership and its impotence.

To complete this list:

- Forty years of U.S. military Middle East buildup.

For an outline of the United States' historical involvement in this Middle Eastern region as it prepared for ground war, we needed to look again at what game the United States had been playing there since the end of World War II.

In Vietnam, I had learned of the ways Vietnamese viewed themselves as products of their history. For the Vietnamese people, nationalism was essentially a reliving of their history, the 1,000 years it took to free themselves of Chinese control and the 100 years it took to be rid of French colonialism.

Here, in the Gulf War, was petroleum imperialism in a fresh military uniform. The European powers had long planted their military markers around the region, ever since the British Royal Navy had converted its battleships from coal burners to oil burners. Now it was the U.S. finger on the trigger that would escalate a foreign claim to that oil's destiny.

"The scale of the U.S. military deployment in the Persian Gulf—half of all U.S. combat forces worldwide—came as something of a shock, even to the Pentagon." So began a March 1 front-page *NCR* article written by Joe Stork and Martha Wenger under a four-column headline "Gulf War: 40 years in the making." Stork and Wenger, editor and assistant editor of *Middle East Report*, specialists in the region, presented a well-researched report that traced direct U.S. military involvement in the region to the CIA's successful covert intervention in Iran in 1953 that overthrew the elected regime of Mohammed Mossadegh and brought the Shah of Iran, Reza Pahlavi, back to power.

They wrote, "Each intervention required a more substantial investment and greater risk than the one before it." Among the points they made were these:

- Washington encouraged U.S. weapons manufacturers to sell $8.3 billion worth of arms to the Shah of Iran between 1970 and 1979, and about 5,000 U.S. advisers helped expand and train his army and secret police.

- Beginning in 1972, with U.S. encouragement and support, Iran provided arms, funds and sanctuary to Iraqi Kurdish rebels fighting against Baghdad.

- The 1979 overthrow of the shah radically changed U.S. strategic planning and moved the United States to quietly begin building multibillion-dollar military ties.

- Between 1970 and 1979, Saudi Arabia had already purchased $3.2 billion worth of U.S. weapons and military services. By 1978, about 675 U.S. military personnel and 10,000 civilian employees of U.S. defense contractors were building military installations in Saudi Arabia.

- Reagan administration Defense Secretary Caspar Weinberger made clear in his 1984-1988 Defense Guidance report that U.S., not Saudi forces, would be the first-line forces in any crisis. "Whatever the circumstances," he wrote, "we should be prepared to introduce American forces directly into the region should it appear that the security of access to Persian Gulf oil is threatened."

- During the 1980s, Saudi Arabia poured nearly $50 billion into building a Gulf-wide air defense system to U.S. and NATO specifications ready for U.S. forces to use in a crisis.

- By 1988, the U.S. Army Corp of Engineers had designed and constructed a $14 billion network of military facilities across Saudi Arabia.

- There was no evidence that Iraq planned to invade Saudi Arabia. The Bush administration intervened militarily in order to offset Iraq's ability to dominate the Gulf politically following a successful and unchallenged conquest of Kuwait.

As far as President Bush's Middle East went, he merely picked up where President Reagan had left off. The United States had invested billions to protect access to Persian Gulf oil and was willing all along to intervene militarily, if necessary. The problem for Bush, however, in the months leading up to the war was that, in the eyes of most Americans, Gulf oil access or cheap petroleum were not sufficient reasons to send U.S. men and women into combat and possible death. More was needed. Fear as a useful domestic tool has already been discussed. We saw the decision made to demonize the strongman Saddam Hussein. For his part, Hussein certainly made it easy. Nevertheless, Saddam Hussein would have to be portrayed as not only a ruthless dictator, but also as a threat to the entire Middle East, if not to every decent and peace-loving American. Bush compared Hussein to Hitler, endlessly spoke of the chemical weapons he used on his own people—never saying the poor Kurds had been encouraged by outsiders, including the CIA, to resist Hussein. The Kurds, used in years past, would once again be used during the Iraq war as temporary tools of U.S. foreign policy: supported one day, discarded the next.

There is a serious object lesson for Americans in this: When economic interests, not human rights, become the basis upon which foreign policy is drawn, human beings become means, or tools, and not ends in their own right. When Bush thought it served his interest, he began quoting an early Amnesty International report that condemned Iraqi actions in Kuwait. The report stated that invading Iraqis unplugged infant incubators in a Kuwaiti hospital, allegedly to send the incubators back to Iraq. After the war, however, it was found that the incubators had never been shipped to Iraq, that they had been found in a hospital back room, and that they had been abandoned after Kuwaiti doctors and nurses fled the country.

The object lesson, of course, is that Bush takes seriously only those Amnesty International reports that suit his purposes and expose his enemies of the moment.

No doubt, Hussein was and is a ruthless leader. But when I was considering what to say about the Iraqi strongman in *NCR* editorials during the war, I was always faced with the Reagan and Bush administrations' track records of demonizing foreign leaders when it served the impulses of U.S. militarism. The success that presidents seem to have in doing this is, for me, one of the most troubling aspects of the war. In 1991, the demon was Saddam Hussein; the year before, it was Manuel Noriega of Panama; before that, Daniel Ortega of Nicaragua; before that, Moammar Gadhafi of Libya and the Ayatollah Khomeini of Iran. Who, I asked myself, will be the new demon in 1992?

The president seemed eager to battle. It was as if he were trying to disprove Doonesbury's Gary Trudeau or to cartoonist Oliphant, who had both ridiculed Bush for being a "wimp." In addition, he eschewed negotiations. For example, when Jordan's King Hussein, a Middle East ally, came to Washington with a peace plan, Bush kept the King waiting for a day in a downtown Washington hotel while he rested at Camp David.

Bush's single-minded, rush-to-war approach to the crisis sparked *NCR* columnist Jesuit Father Robert Drinan to comment in the February 15 issue:

> The president, trying to turn the war into a religious crusade, demonizes Saddam to such a degree that he degrades those who, for profoundly religious reasons, want to deal with Saddam by nonviolent means. . . .

> Even a cursory study of the complexities of the Middle East promptly yields the conclusion that the defeat of one leader by intense violence cannot bring peace to a troubled area; indeed, it might well aggravate and intensify the age-old quarrels that are legendary in the Arab world.

> Even a superficial examination of the causes of the war will make clear that the protesters say it well in one of their placards: "No death for oil." Bush senses the thrust of that adage and continually states the United States is fighting for a cause that is noble, moral and divinely directed.

Bush succeeded. He used television. Each day as he spoke, he knew his words would be picked up on the evening news. He quickly took control of the discussions. He shaped the issues. He decided what was important, what was not. Daily themes were worked out by his media planners. The lessons of theme control, learned during his election campaign, were extended to fit this first major international crisis of his presidential term. Stirring up fear became Bush's most useful tool to win public support for his war policy. Hussein, we learned, was a madman and, further, he was soon to possess nuclear weapons. This caught the public's attention. War fever grew. It was working. Bush had found a reason to fight now and not wait to see if sanctions might work. In the process, he muzzled Congress. It dared not take from him the support he claimed he needed to protect U.S. soldiers in the Gulf from Hussein's nuclear potential. U.S. intelligence, meanwhile, privately never believed Hussein would soon have the Bomb or the means to deliver a nuclear warhead. They were estimating he might need up to a decade, if not more. Never mind that *that* story got buried inside the newspapers. To listen to Bush, one would think Hussein could have a nuclear arsenal within a month or two.

"Every day," the president warned the nation solemnly, Saddam was getting closer to the day he would have the Bomb. True. And clever. It revealed the Bush mind-set, a man intent on destroying the last defenses of the Democratic Party's "give-sanctions-a-chance" opposition. Once the sanctions option had been discarded and the bombings begun, the ground war would be the logical conclusion. Its time was coming. By mid-February the U.S. public was ready and willing—even eager—to have it out with Saddam Hussein on the ground.

The anti-Hussein and anti-Iraqi hysteria was, meanwhile, having another troubling side effect throughout the country. Anti-Arab feelings were on the rise. The American-Arab Anti-Discrimination Committee reported in early February that hate crimes against Arab-Americans had increased "nearly a hundredfold" in six months since the Iraqi invasion of Kuwait. These human-rights abuses only added to the sadness of those days and caused many to reflect back to World War II, when Americans of Japanese descent were rounded up and placed in concentration camps along the West Coast. The Bush administration added to Arab-American hardships by allowing the FBI to interview, indeed interrogate, Arab-Americans—allegedly to thwart terrorism.

But Arab-Americans looked at it differently. *NCR* interviewed a number of those Arab-Americans at the time, including key leaders of their three largest U.S. organizations. One of the most articulate was Jim Zogby, president of the Arab-American Institute, who castigated the administration for the FBI interviews. "Imagine if they (the FBI) went into a Knights of Columbus meeting and started asking questions about the Irish Republican Army, or if they asked members of the Sons of Italy about the Mafia," Zogby said, estimating that the FBI had conducted 200 to 300 interviews.

One of the saddest stories we published at the time was that of a Seton Hall University basketball player, Marco Lokar, an Italian who refused to wear a U.S. flag on his basketball uniform and, as a result, was subjected, along with his pregnant wife, to local harassment. "From a Christian standpoint, I cannot support any war, with no exception for the Persian Gulf War," Lokar said, before leaving Seton Hall and returning to his hometown in Italy.

But every last doubt that a modern war could be fought within certain "rules of conduct" seemed to evaporate during those heady days as key administration members and supporters began to talk about the possible retaliatory use of tactical nuclear weapons against Iraq. It was astonishing. I asked my staff how seriously our paper ought to consider this talk. In the end, we figured that whether or not it was seriously intended, the fact that it was being said deserved to be printed. So we wrote about it. To hear U.S. officials speak so cavalierly about using nuclear weapons, one wondered if they had just awakened from a 40-year sleep. It also revealed yet more signs of the nation's growing hysteria, a pathology seemingly infecting the whole body politic.

What started the United States on this course? How did the infection become so serious in such a short time? These were some of the questions we asked and answered in various different ways in the months leading up to the war. We never came up with complete or definitive answers, but in our newsroom discussions, our search for answers led us back to the changing U.S. relationship with the Soviet Union. As one long time *NCR* columnist, Thomas Blackburn, had written, the post-Cold War era seems to have all the disadvantages of the Cold War with none of the advantages— like restraint. We saw in Bush administration statements and actions a sense of new possibilities and many, we feared, could lead to further U.S. military action. Would Cuba be next? The late U.S. Senator William Fulbright of Arkansas, head of the Senate Foreign Relations Committee during the Vietnam War and an articulate critic of the Vietnam War, wrote a book titled *The Arrogance of Power*. This arrogance, he argued, leads to reckless U.S. military adventurism overseas. The term has stuck in my mind all these years. I think the Bush White House had become infected by this arrogance, especially since the fall of the Berlin Wall in October of 1989.

Defense Secretary Richard Cheney, asked about using nuclear weapons, said, "We don't rule options in or out." Vice President Dan Quayle, who had never been in a war, said knowingly: "You never rule any options out." Meanwhile, *NCR* Washington Bureau Chief Joe Feuerherd reported in *NCR*'s February 22 issue that Washington, D.C.'s, Army-Navy Club had scheduled a debate for the following week. The topic: "Should Iraq be Nuked?" Important and powerful segments of the nation were either sick or had lost their senses in a matter of a few weeks. I couldn't figure out which was worse. The media was not helping. It, too, seemingly had become infected, though the symptoms were different. Local television particularly, but the national networks increasingly, bought into the war, hopelessly losing any ability to maintain critical distance from events. They had become cheerleaders for the administration.

No doubt, books will be written about press conduct during this sad episode in U.S. journalism. I cannot see how much of the media will escape the judgment that it abrogated many of its First Amendment responsibilities. Much of the media became hoodwinked and muzzled at the same time. But how did the president pull it off? We know that the Pentagon felt it lost the Vietnam War because domestic support eroded back home. I thank the heavens it did.

We knew by this time that the Pentagon knew it was necessary to control war coverage, as in Grenada and Panama. But from personal observation, press coverage appeared to weaken even further once Bush ordered the first U.S. troops to the Middle East. That's when the broadcasters began to focus on the families of those being sent. The national media carried the pain of those separations, the vulnerability of the soldiers, their spouses and children left behind. From there, widespread sentiments quickly moved to "We must support our troops" and then to "we support our troops." The yellow ribbons came out by the tens of thousands. So did the flags. Americans tried to outdo one another in public displays of patriotism. At the paper, we asked how long the support would have lasted had Bush called upon the nation to make personal sacrifices, such as paying a war tax. The answer, we agreed, was, not long. The fact that Bush did not ask for a special tax indicates he felt the same way we did about the matter.

Once America was in full support of its troops in the Gulf, questioning U.S. Gulf policy could be viewed as a sign of betrayal. This was completely illogical, of course. War protesters met the problem head on. Many carried placards saying: "Support U.S. troops. . . . *Bring them home from the Gulf!*" Fearing any appearance of being out of step with popular sentiment, television stations began to compete to see which one could do the most heart-rending human interest story.

This is not to say American sentiments were all badly placed. Most were genuine. But they were manipulated by the administration for its own ends. Meanwhile, the national media gave virtually no serious coverage to the antiwar protesters, whether they were in the streets or on university campuses. Instead, each network, seeking analysis, placed ex-generals and ex-admirals on contract and turned to them daily to give meaning to events in the Middle East. It was all very cozy. But was it good journalism? What had happened to independent journalists who worked the Pentagon corridors night and day to develop sources more interested in shedding light on events than doing simple public relations for their former colleagues and bosses? As war sentiment grew, the last semblance of policy debate faded from our television screens.

Self-censorship became more common. Before it was over, practically the only thing being debated on television was the exact week of the month that U.S. ground troops ought to enter Kuwait. By then, there was only one view of what needed to be done. It was summarized in two words heard throughout the country. The United States, it was said, had to "kick butt."

Back in Saudi Arabia, the press corps could learn almost nothing about the what was going on. The military accompanied reporters on brief supervised pool trips to the front line or to an aircraft carrier, where nothing essential could be learned but where "photo opportunities" were good. A few correspondents, angered and frustrated by the unprecedented censorship (among them CBS's Bob Simon, who had been in Vietnam and was old enough to remember what real war reporting required), ventured out on their own. That he was captured by Iraqi soldiers and held until the war's end did not in any way make his decision less worthy or valid—although that was the lesson the U.S. military wanted everyone to believe. Virtually nothing we learned from the Middle East during those days did not first pass through some military censor. While all this censorship was allegedly being done to protect the troops and battle plans, few believed it. It was unnerving to sit in my office and read dispatches in my daily *New York Times* that indicated the material had passed through military censors.

When the Pentagon announced that the press would not be permitted to film the return of U.S. soldiers' bodies shipped back from the Middle East, it was clear this censorship had taken on aspects of domestic propaganda-by-default in a manner that went well beyond any desire to keep information from the enemy. That is, of course, unless the U.S. military also viewed the U.S. public as its enemy. (An argument could be made that the Pentagon considers a public aroused by body bags and casualty counts just that—an enemy!)

Something fundamental had gone wrong in the media. It was letting the military and administration dictate its preferences. And we all knew something had gone wrong. These thoughts led to the following remarks, which appeared in an editorial in our February 22 issue:

> In the Gulf War, both sides are censoring, controlling and suppressing journalists, the U.S. military to a degree unsurpassed in the history of war reporting in this country.
>
> What is worse, millions of Americans are cheering that suppression on, and some are calling for even more. Their motives may be patriotic, but when you wrap yourself in a flag, it is hard to see. They may sense what the allied command tells them is the need of military security, but the political underbelly of it all goes undetected.
>
> The United States lost the war in Vietnam, and both the administration and the military—committing the age-old mistake of blaming the messenger rather than the message—blame the media for part of the loss.
>
> They fear that too much public exposure to the realities of war would cost them the political support they need to wage it.
>
> So they all but gag (and even physically detain) the only people who could give an accurate report of that reality, the

journalists, and we let them do it. How easily we let our freedom go.

Sometimes we go even further than that. Sometimes—as when we call for a greater suppression of journalists so this nation can wage war more easily in support of anti-democratic forces—we give it away.

By mid-February we were receiving much feedback from our readers concerning *NCR*'s war-related coverage. The letters were generally positive. Some readers even phoned to say they appreciated *NCR* those weeks because it made them realize they were not "crazy" for thinking the way they did about the war. Some sample letters:

There is no time to explain. I simply have to thank you for your consistent, sane, clear-eyed and Christian exploration and analysis of the current madness in the United States and the Persian Gulf.

— Mary Ellen Neill, Lexington, Ky.

As I read the bishops' reactions to the Gulf War, I grew more depressed and outraged. A new luxury has been added to the morally schizophrenic church-teaching, the just-war theory.

— Darleene White, Edina, Minn.

. . . The clear, present and future danger faced by the world in general, and the United States in particular, has little to do with the ruthless despot Saddam Hussein or even with East-West superpower polarities. It has more to do with rich-versus-poor, North-South polarities as well as an interrelated polarity, between human activities and the life-sustaining capacities of Earth. . . .

— Frank G. Splitt, Mt. Prospect, Ill.

Of course, not everyone loved us:

Appropriately, your most recent editions have been dedicated to the war in the Persian Gulf. It's the first time that
such a grand chorus of authors writing from "Lalaland" has
been assembled. Almost to a woman/man, each has written as if Saddam Hussein and his behavior were a figment
of the collective American imagination. . . .

— (Msgr.) Robert J. Ennis, Fort Carson, Colo.

Meanwhile, what had become of the nation's moral leaders?
What about the church leadership? To be sure, this was a war most
definitely fought without the blessings of the top leadership in
most of the nation's churches. However, at the local level, especially as the nation readied itself to go to battle, opposition from
priests and ministers was spotty, at best. The country had been
steamrolled into the war and most local churches went down with
everyone else. The higher-ups continued to deplore the bombings,
criticize policies, express remorse, call for prayers—but most took
no outright actions to oppose the conflict. Either they feared going
too public or did not know what to do. Almost none of the U.S.
archbishops went to the heart of the matter and actually condemned the war. Doing so might have meant having to advise
Gulf-bound soldiers to stay at home. Then again, some bishops felt
obligated to state their own moral conclusions about the war while
telling others they would have to come to conclusions of their
own. This approach suited those who felt the final decisions had to
rest within the consciences of the faithful.

One day in our office in a discussion about the war, a staff
member pointed out that the bishops, having condemned abortion,
had come out favoring specific actions, including the support of
proposed legislation, to end or limit abortions. In other words,
they had gone from word to deed. On the Gulf issue, however,
they were still for the most part in the "word" stage. The staffer
didn't think it likely the bishops would go beyond that point.

Anchorage Archbishop Francis Hurley stood out from most others. He condemned the war as immoral. Others had lots to say

against it but withheld outright condemnation. They often preferred to warn the nation and, presumably, U.S. officials that for
the war to be deemed "just," it would have to be fought within the
framework of just-war teachings. In other words, the war had to be
fought with regard for protecting noncombatants and through pro-
portional means.

The U.S. military, of course, would argue it was doing everything it could to contain the violence and to avoid needless deaths.
The videos of laser-guided bombs and assurances by military briefers indicated a military concern that civilians were not dying in
large numbers. Many church leaders seemed assured. Jesuit Father
Bryan Hehir, consultant to the U.S. bishops' conference, told *NCR*
that "it was remarkable the way in which the official government
pronouncements want to respond to the (just-war) questions. The
language is there." To the degree that church leaders were critical,
those criticisms were not generally being heard by the American
people. Voices of criticism could not be heard above the chorus of
war chants coming from the administration. If the church leadership had wanted to step out and assert itself, it would have had to
work together and act boldly. There was little indication at the
time that they would do either.

At the paper, it seemed to us that the die had been cast. I
thought that it was too late and that, if the churches had acted to
stop the war, they would have had to act before the bombings
began. Once into that dark night, it was all over. What had disappointed me and others on our staff was the unwillingness of most
church leaders, the bishops included, to press for deeper ex-
planations. Was it a war for oil or was it not? It seemed so obvious
that going to war "to protect U.S. interests" half a world away
called for serious moral examination and explanation. At a minimum, it seemed that the Catholic bishops, if they had wanted to
examine the morality of the buildup, ought to have held special
hearings to get a fix on U.S. foreign policy in the Middle East.

Since the 1960s, many Christians here and around the world
have been talking about "structural sin." Many of the new theolo-

gies coming out of Latin America and Asia in the past two decades have examined economics in the light of Gospel teachings. Pope John Paul II, in an emotional speech in Canada in September 1984, stated: "The poor people and the poor nations—poor in different ways, not only lacking in food, but also deprived of freedom and other human rights—will judge those people who take their goods away from them, amassing to themselves the imperialistic monopoly of economic and military supremacy at the expense of others." The Catholic Church increasingly recognizes that some forms of sin stem from unjust structures and selfish economic and military policies. That's why it was particularly disappointing for me that more U.S. bishops did not probe more deeply into these "background" questions as they attempted to assess the war and pass judgment on it.

Some bishops, however, did raise these broader, war-related questions. At a talk in Kansas City, Missouri, to a packed audience in a Catholic high-school auditorium, Detroit Auxiliary Bishop Thomas Gumbleton condemned the war, saying it was immoral to fight a war, as Bush had once said, to "preserve the American way of life."

One of the more disappointing moments of the war came for me in my office one day as I read Chicago Cardinal Joseph Bernardin's moral assessment of the conflict. As principal episcopal author of the 1983 U.S. bishops' peace pastoral, the cardinal's assessment would be viewed as having particular importance. Essentially, he wrote that he had concluded that the war was "just" but not "wise." This explanation of Bernardin's remarks and NCR's reaction to his remarks appeared as an editorial in the March 1 issue:

> (Bernardin) wrote that he opposed the war in mid-January because he was convinced at the time that other means of resolving the conflict had not been exhausted. He went on to admit that, as the prospect of a ground war approached, he was having "greater doubts about (the war's) long-term implications," yet was "not prepared to state cat-

egorically, as some have, that it is unjust or immoral." He went on to say that, "even if it can be legitimately argued that the just-war criteria are substantially fulfilled, I continue to question the wisdom of going to war when we did."

In sum, the Gulf War is probably just, but unwise. Bernardin shows us that he is clearly anguished about the war and shares honest doubt about its morality. Many Catholics share his doubts. But we are left wondering.

Has not the church long taught that when there is doubt, the strong presumption must always be on the side of life? This is, after all, the foundation of the church's strong anti-abortion teaching. Life must be presumed and protected from conception on.

Further, have not church just-war principles taught us that the initial presumption is that all wars are unjust—unless proven otherwise? That is why we are left wondering why Bernardin wrote that he was not prepared to state categorically that this war is unjust or immoral.

Given Catholic teachings, would Bernardin not have been on far more sound theological ground to have written: "It seems a land war is likely, and I begin to have greater doubts about its long-tern implications. I am not prepared to state categorically, as some have, that it is just or moral?" Why, we ask, must the burden of proof always fall upon the peacemakers?

Bernardin's assessment reminded me of some of the hair-splitting the bishops went through in their 1983 pastoral. Broadly speaking, it was a success in that it committed the church to pursue peace as never before. Yet, as far as I was concerned, in its specific assessment of nuclear deterrence it failed tragically. After considerable examination of nuclear weapons and nuclear deterrence, the bishops concluded that, practically speaking, it would be immoral to use them in war.

But they faced a problem. To flatly condemn their *use* would imply the further conclusion that to *possess* them would also be immoral, and if *possession* were immoral, then to *manufacture* them would be immoral. Were the bishops willing to take on the entire nuclear weapons industry? We at the paper thought that this is precisely what was required of them. But the bishops concluded otherwise, arguing that it is theoretically possible to use a nuclear weapon discriminately on, say, a battleship at sea. Theoretical use gave the bishops a way out. Neat and quite rational. But did it speak in any manner to what Jesus had to say about love of enemy and forgiveness? We did not think so. And we thought the bishops had missed an opportunity to break once and for all with the just-war tradition, a tradition that seemed to us and a growing number of other Catholics to no longer make sense, given the weapons of modern war.

Bernardin's nuclear assessment in 1983 and his assessment of the Gulf War in 1991 can be said to take the church a good way down the peace path from two decades back but, in my opinion, can also be viewed as fundamentally flawed, or at least, unwilling to take that critical step required by faith in the light of the Gospels. The "justified" killings of 100,000 or more Iraqis in a month of bombings should be sufficient evidence for the prosecution to send the just-war theory into church history books alongside other long-discarded teachings, such as the belief that only men had souls.

All that was going on in February, *before* the ground war. Bush had a free hand. Bombings continued around the clock. B-52s were flying in from Europe and bases in the Middle East to pound Hussein's Republican Guards. Events were moving rapidly and there was so much we did not know. As we worked on the weekly issue in the Kansas City newsroom, we kept a television on, sound turned low. We glanced up from time to time to look at CNN's ongoing war coverage. We waited with a strong sense that more was coming. We realize now that the worst was yet to come.

10

Bombs Falling Slowly

Stop.

The mind does not comprehend. There are times when words interfere, as the Chinese mystic Lao-tzu warned. There are times when words do not suffice. The moment demands the attention of our whole being. Faced with comprehending a *war* and *bombing*, we must slow down for a few moments. This is not melodrama; this is life and death we are facing, discussing, comprehending, attempting to absorb. This is reality. So jaded have we become that we are apt to brush past this violence as if it were just another headline or news item.

We must be seated and conscious of where we sit. We must breathe in slowly. Sit in silence. Be conscious of our breathing. It keeps us alive. Be still. . . .

Now, slowly, quietly, we can let our being, our imagination come alive. Follow me to a rice field in the Mekong Delta. Or to a desert sand dune in Iraq. Listen to the silence. We feel the air against our skin. The silence comes from the plants, from the sand. They are part of creation. We, too, are part of creation. Alive. Breathing. Hear the silence of the still air, muggy or dry. The silence speaks. Slowly, very slowly, look up into the dark, blue sky, open and clear, a reflection of the sunlight that supports all life we know. We see nothing but the rich and open blues in that warm and giving sky.

But wait . . . up there in that blue . . . the tiniest of objects are coming into sight. Bombs are falling. Transformed, we are a Vietnamese peasant. We are the Iraqi mother with child in arms. We see the bombs dropping . . . dropping silently from above. These are American bombs, powerful bombs. They are deadly and they are falling. We begin to hear their shrieks. Vaguely . . . and now more loudly and louder still. The sound grows quickly now, louder and louder. It is suddenly deafening. They are striking now, pounding against the earth, one after another after another, blasting and spitting up everything around us. Our ears are throbbing, pounding, splitting open. The bombs are falling now directly upon us. This split-second is eternal. We are alone, cut off from all we have ever known—family, friends, children, plants, sun, moon, stars, hopes, dreams, prayers. . . . Silence. Darkness. Sit still in the darkness. Share the death. Share the sorrow. Share the lost tomorrows. . . .

Return to this world now. Leave the imaginary bombs behind. We have plenty of real ones.

Forgive me for this exercise. It comes out of my frustration. We in the West cannot know. Our minds do not comprehend. We can measure precisely the explosive force of U.S. bombs. We sell bombs by the pound. We can count the megatonnage. Calculate the outer range of certain death. But we do not know, not really. I am convinced we do not know. I refuse to believe we Americans know. If we knew, we would not pay for these bombs. We would not drop them on foreign peoples to keep U.S. oil prices low. We would not feel proud to have dropped them. Not the good Americans I know. I believe if we really knew what our bombs do, we would all scream: "No, no, no! Not in my name! Not one more bomb!"

The East knows what the West does not. In the East, spirituality constitutes real power. Emptiness is understood.

In the West, technology has become our god. It fills us. It offers precious fruits. But at a deadly cost. The cost of enlightenment. If there is no room for emptiness, nothing can be filled. We cannot understand. The South knows when the North does not. In the South, poverty and oppression have made survival a daily goal. A grain of rice is understood. The barrel of the gun is pointed at my face, my family. Powerlessness opens the soul to essential truth. Solidarity is possible. Required. In the North, fast cars, full bellies and TV commercials slide day into day and year into year. Follow the fashions. The banquet of life is assumed. Communion is lost! The bombs are shipped overseas . . . and forgotten. Truth is of little matter. So how can we know? How do I convey the feelings, sights and sounds of the bombs I heard dropped in Vietnam. How do I relate the stories of those who lived through the bombings and those who did not? The United States dropped 4.6 million tons of bombs upon Vietnam. What does it mean? Two million Vietnamese died in the war. We left and forgot. What does it mean? Should I stop telling my stories? Some 100,000, perhaps 150,000 or more died in the Gulf War. What does it mean? We leave. Will we forget? Who will speak out? Who will beg for forgiveness?

Throughout the war against Iraq there was much talk about "just" and "unjust" wars. There was talk of "proportionality," as if the gift of life, a gift of the Creator, could somehow be contained, measured and quantified. It is as if we, the creatures of the creation, dared become the Creator to hold some heavenly scale in our hands. With it we could weigh justice, make judgment, participate in the execution.

Was the Gulf War moral by "just-war" criteria. If the Iraqis killed 5,000 Kuwaitis, does the war to liberate Kuwait become disproportionately evil if 6,000 Iraqi civilians die? What about 10,000? 50,000? 100,000? 150,000? If only 100 Americans died, then does this lesser cost weigh on the side of making the war more moral? In coming to judgment, does an American death count the same as an Iraqi? Can we know, really know, the intention of our government? Were U.S. intentions selfless? Does, then, evil exist only according to intention in the mind? What information do we have to make moral judgments? Can the United States or any government be believed as it prepares to go to war? Do we understand our own propaganda? Can we see it for what it is? Or is part of the nature of successful propaganda the ability to hide what it is?

All of us, as U.S. citizens, are failing to understand the nature of U.S. militarism in the late 20th century. Sometimes, we are blinded by the good people we know who are part of the U.S. armed forces. The evil stems not from the hearts of these people, but rather from decades of policies aimed at achieving some kind of antiquated "national security" long after the planet has entered the global age. To continue the pursuit of "national security," as it has been defined through U.S. foreign policies in recent decades, is, in fact, to assure that the United States will never be truly "secure." There will always be another war to fight to protect U.S. control of an open supply of increasingly dwindling resources. The United States must rejoin the global family with a spirit of cooperation. It must end its aspirations, which mock its democratic traditions and instincts, to "control" the destiny of the planet. It must finally recognize that to work for justice abroad is to work for peace and justice at home.

For U.S. Christians, something else is also at work here. It speaks to a collective effort we need to make at this time in our nation's history to work to save our very own souls and to *live* the beliefs we profess. No one should be more contrary witnesses to war than followers of Christ, who lived and spoke nonviolence and forgiveness and love of enemies. When it comes to war, we must finally embrace that "entirely new attitude" toward war, of which the bishops spoke at the Vatican Council. I believe it will never come if we follow the measurements and measured violence contained in "just-war" theory and responses. No, war must be rejected, period! Nonviolence is the practical response to violence. It is also the Christian faith response to violence. We must become well practiced in nonviolent conflict resolution skills.

We can and must choose to walk another path, to affirm the Infinite. Notice the sacred in all that is. Find power in powerlessness. Open our hearts. And hear the silence of those falling bombs. We must recognize those sins of ours that helped release those bombs. We can discover truth in darkness and overcome that darkness. The Resurrection is contained within the Cross.

As you can see, the war against Iraq was very much a desert experience for me. It was for many others as well. We suffered through the war—but in no way as did its many Middle East victims.

With these desert thoughts in mind, let us return now to the beginning of Lent, February 13, at a point when the war was about to reach its bloodiest stages. None of us was ready for what was about to happen next.

It was Ash Wednesday. I awakened, as I do most days, to catch the news on National Public Radio. Quickly, I learned that a bomb shelter containing many civilians in downtown Baghdad had been hit by two U.S. bombs, killing large but still unconfirmed numbers of people. I flipped on the television to broadcasts from Baghdad showing burned bodies being pulled from the smoldering wreckage. Hundreds, we were told, were still in the shelter with no sign of life yet. Rescue efforts were continuing and would take considerable time to complete. We were also told that these were not stray bombs. This was no accident. These were guided bombs and were direct hits.

That day the war came home—or at least into our homes. It could no longer be denied that innocents were dying in large numbers beneath U.S. bombs. Yet within hours Washington would be releasing statements aimed at diminishing, if not dismissing, its culpability. We were told the deaths were, in fact, the responsibility of Saddam Hussein. He had allowed these civilians to huddle in a military command bunker, hoping it would get bombed so that he could stage a public relations bonanza.

Whatever the case, this was human tragedy on a large scale— and visible for the world to see. For the Iraqi government, which

for days had been trying to publicize the growing numbers of civilian casualties caused by the unrelenting bombings, it was useful.
For the U.S. government, which had been trying to depict the
bombings as "clean" and "surgical," it came as a public relations
nightmare. Even as the covered corpses lay there on a Baghdad
street, these dead had simply become more pawns in a battle between Bush and Hussein. But the bombings did underscore a truth
about the war that the White House for months had ignored and
was now being forced to acknowledge: Beneath the military battle,
another had long existed. It was a battle for interpretation, for
meaning. How would the war be recorded in the minds of millions
around the world, especially the Arab world? Bush had never ac-
knowledged what many others had long said, that he could "win"
the military war—there was never much doubt he could have his
way by force—but in the process, the United States could suffer a
resounding political defeat. This second war, the war over meaning, was highlighted as never before as the press combed through
the Baghdad wreckage for information.

The first thing I did that morning after coming to work was to
make sure *NCR* media-watcher Raymond Schroth was following
events. He said he would do a report for the next issue. His piece
in the March 1 issue focused on the press coverage the incident
received and the "news spin" Washington quickly put on it:

> I watched and listened to the news all day and studied
> seven Thursday papers from around the country for a sense
> of how America received and interpreted these deaths.

> Two quotes from wire services, which appeared in sev-
> eral papers, stand out:

> "As reporters watched, the decapitated body of a
> woman was carried out and laid next to a small torso—
> apparently that of a girl whose head and limbs had been
> blown off." A 17-year-old, a burn victim who woke up
> with his blanket in flames, recounts: "I turned to try to
> touch my mother who was next to me, but grabbed noth-

ing but a piece of flesh." . . . Powerful images—but fleeting. What stands out the most from hours monitoring the tube is CNN bending over backward to almost apologize for what it was showing, reminding us that Peter Arnett's reports were cleared by Iraqi censors—even though, as we learned later, the Iraqis had given the correspondents whom they had bused to the site free rein to report everything they heard and saw. . . .

The administration and its lackeys played two songs: 1. "Blame Saddam." We have evidence, they said, that this was a command and communications center, although they did not present the evidence. And neighborhood people told reporters on the scene that everyone had been using this shelter, which had been built as a shelter during the Iran-Iraq war, since the bombing began. Saddam Hussein is the "kind of man"—according to (Dick) Cheney, Marlin Fitzwater and Pentagon briefer General Thomas Kelly—who would gas his own people, etc. "Saddam Hussein," says Fitzwater, "does not share our value in the sanctity of life." Therefore, he deliberately and secretly put these civilians into this bunker with the hope that we would kill them and give him an issue to exploit.

But George Bush—they did not say—is also the "kind of man" who, without blinking, was willing to kill hundreds of Panamanian civilians to "arrest" General Noriega, who had once been on his CIA payroll but now had pushed his presidential patience too far. A lot of the "collateral damage" to Baghdad, Cheney told the cheering Chamber, was also the fault of the Iraqis themselves: The antiaircraft shells they shot at our bombers fell to earth and hit their homes. His logic seemed to be that the next time our bombers came over, they should simply let them bomb away.

2. "Blame Peter Arnett." Remember, Kelly said again and again, perhaps not knowing that Arnett had been free,

the CNN information from Baghdad (unlike that from the Pentagon and Saudi Arabia?) emanated from a "controlled press." . . . Perhaps the most depressing aftermath of the Ash Wednesday bombing has been the dominant tone of the "moral" commentary—the apparent consensus that since civilian deaths are "inevitable," we bear no responsibility for them.

Columnist George Will frankly spells out that, when Americans voted for war, they voted for the substantial civilian casualties that are implicit in U.S. strategy. The 20th century's moral abyss, he says, beckons when "long-range killing gives rise to abstractness about its consequences." But he does not say we should stop. *The Washington Post*'s Charles Krauthammer blames both Saddam and Peter Arnett. "Saddam's strategy is one which the Palestinians have perfected over the last decade: Provoke a fight, lose the fight, pile up the bodies and invite the press." We simply have to steel our nerves, he says, and look at the bodies without being distracted by guilt.

He does not tell us, by the way, how many bodies the Palestinians, having lost their *intifadah* fights with the Israelis, have had to pile up. Answer: 900. But of all the reports, images and debates of Ash Wednesday 1991, the one sentence that will remain with me is the BBC reporter describing the smoking corpses being toted out from underground. "Many," he said, "were barely recognizable as human." That seems to have been the idea.

The bombings had to stop, we felt. Looking back, I have to admit it was preposterous to expect that Bush would consider calling off the bombing. It was just as absurd to think he would decide to end hostilities and return to the lesser path of waiting for sanctions to take their toll. Who within the White House or Pentagon was listening to anyone not supportive of Bush's war policies? Certainly, the administration would pay no attention to a newspaper that, pointing to the Baghdad killings, would demand: "Stop the bombing!" Yet, as an editor, I am called upon to speak out, to speak my mind as honestly and openly as I can. There was no one in our newsroom who did not want the bombings ended immediately. This was not just about policy. This was about morality.

Sometimes, one writes even if the powers that be are not listening. Maybe especially if they are not listening. And if no one hears today, then possibly someone will at some time in the distant future. And that person might take heart from knowing what was said many years back. That person, or persons, may be encouraged to know some Americans were speaking out against the folly, against the madness.

Just after the bombings began, we published a front-page editorial with the future in mind. The editorial in our January 25 issue stated: "We have promised to teach the next generation. . . . If within our lives, nation and world violence still reigns, the path of nonviolence is no less correct. Our efforts remain firm, our eyes— and hopes—fixed upon our children and those generations still to come."

Remembering those words, the editorial we wrote for our February 22 issue in the wake of the Baghdad killings—even if Washington and much of the nation were not listening at the time—makes sense:

> . . . Whatever legal foundation this war has rests upon the U.N. mandate, and that mandate authorizes the use of force to liberate Kuwait. Nothing more. Not the devastation of Iraq. Not the removal of Saddam Hussein. The continuing ferocity of the U.S.-led air attack against urban areas, long after most even marginally military targets have been hit over and over, has soared well beyond the horizons of the U.N. mandate. It is time to stop.
>
> Nations, especially since the advent of aerial bombardment, have often tried to break the will of their enemies by

killing civilians. Remember Dresden. Remember Hiroshima. Remember Hanoi.

Peer through the dust of that historic debris, it is worth
remembering that, though it may have assembled a big military machine, Iraq is a small country. It has only about 18
million people (before the West started slaughtering them,
at least). Half of that population is under age 18—thanks,
in part, to the war with Iran. At least five million Iraqis are
under 5 years old. That, too, is Iraq. Is last week's slaughter
in the Baghdad bunker what happens when the military is
given its head? The U.S. military blames its loss in Vietnam
on press publicity and political constraint, but it should be
clear to everyone by now that war is too deadly serious to
be left to the military alone. Especially in a democratic nation. Far more than the future of Kuwait or the future of
Iraq is at risk here. How long will it be before Americans
realize once again that the bombs they drop on foreign
lands fall on the home front as well? It is time to stop the
bombing, stop the war, return to more civilized—to say
nothing of more moral and more reasonable—ways of dealing with Saddam Hussein. Not for his sake. Or even for
Iraq's. But for our own.

We were all glued to our televisions, especially early on. The
longer the war continued, the more television watching became a
professional chore. It needs to be noted that, for all the destruction
we brought down upon Iraq, we saw little of the results of U.S.
actions. The Pentagon occasionally shared with us videos of precisely targeted bombs. Of course, it kept from us the 70 percent,
revealed after the war, that never hit their targets. Given the military mind-set, one might have expected as much from the Pentagon. More shocking, however, was that given the opportunity to
air footage of civilian damage and casualties in Iraq, the networks
turned down the offer. They simply decided not to. Their decisions

constituted outrageous self-censorship and spoke legions about much of the media's general acquiescence and then support for the war effort.

For example, NBC had access to raw, uncensored footage of Iraqi victims that it had planned to air February 12 on the "Today" show and on the nightly news, but the broadcast was canceled. The network also ended its 12-year association with the independent filmmaker, Jon Alpert, saying it would no longer accept his free-lance work. The footage recorded his travels inside Iraq with former U.S. Attorney General Ramsey Clark. They were able to take hours of videotape of civilian deaths and destruction caused by the bombings.

When we heard of NBC's decision, *NCR* staff writer Demetria Martinez began to investigate. Her piece, which appeared in our March 15 issue, revealed that officials at the major networks, each citing different reasons, concluded the video was not "newsworthy." According to an article in the March 4, 1991, issue of *Variety*, an international entertainment weekly, NBC News President Michael Gartner, who never saw the footage, decided against using it and severed Alpert's relationship with the network. The article said Gartner did this because Alpert had years earlier staged footage of the American ambassador lowering the flag over the Kabul, Afghanistan, embassy—a decision Alpert later admitted was a mistake. Nevertheless, Alpert had undertaken several NBC assignments since. Another NBC official said Alpert's connection with Clark presented another problem. "We didn't want it to look like we were associated with Clark's mission. We're not going to prostitute ourselves like that," NBC official Don Brown said.

In doing our own article on the controversy, we decided it was germane to mention that since 1986 NBC has been owned by General Electric, one of the top U.S. defense contractors and that this had led to some media critic claims that NBC could not be trusted vigorously to pursue some war-related stories. Alpert told *NCR* that NBC official Gartner wanted "to avoid any controversy at all costs." Alpert said, "He didn't want NBC associated with the

Ramsey Clarks of the world." Alpert said he stressed that he was "independent" of Clark but that traveling with him gave the group he was with wide access to Iraq.

CBS and CNN also turned down offers to air the footage, which eventually got onto New York's PBS affiliate and MTV news. Brian Becker, a staff member of the National Coalition to Stop U.S. Intervention in the Middle East, which Clark had helped to found, said the video showed that the claim of "surgical bombing was a farce." Indeed, the footage showed one neighborhood so devastated by U.S. bombs aimed at a bridge that the neighbors had considered blowing up the bridge themselves in order to halt further bombings. We felt that these were among the more important stories to come out, but they received almost no press coverage in the dailies during the war.

The bombing, meanwhile, grew in intensity as the ground war approached. B-52s were being used to hit the Republican Guard, the elite Iraqi troops, using cluster bombs and 1,000-pound bombs. The Soviet Union led some last-ditch, international efforts to negotiate Iraq's withdrawal from Kuwait. In retrospect, it was a move that, had it been given a chance to succeed, could have saved tens of thousands of lives and immeasurable environmental damage within Kuwait. However, Hussein hesitated and Bush wanted none of it. The administration, it seemed at the time, could taste the blood and was ready to drink.

It all happened quickly, almost all of it completely out of sight of media pool teams, which during the four days of actual ground combat were kept a day or two away from the most serious encounters. What came out was a mirage, the *appearance* of an aggressive press on hand as public witness, but this was not the reality. Part of the reason, certainly, for the noncoverage had to do with the quick pace at which events were moving. However, journalists are accustomed to that. In any case, the result was that the U.S. military had a free hand to "get the job done" without the prying eyes of reporters or camera crews recording *what* the military was actually doing to get the job done. Before we knew it, the battles were almost over and General Norman Schwarzkopf was lifting the veil. He stood before maps and briefing charts, his victorious battle plan revealed.

Press reports indicated that there had been little Iraqi resistance. Iraqi soldiers, outnumbered, outclassed, outarmed and without air cover, retreated quickly to the north into Iraq. Pursued and outflanked by allied tanks, armored personnel carriers and helicopter gunships, the Iraqi retreat quickly became a rout. Even more U.S. air power was called in—and then silence.

We woke up a day later to front-page pictures of what appeared to be a ghost caravan stretching, some said, seven miles along the road out of Kuwait City toward Basra. It was an eerie site. Hundreds, maybe thousands, of buses, trucks and cars twisted, broken and charred, scattered about, generally facing north. But with few exceptions—a few burned bodies hanging out the sides of a few trucks—there were no people. There were no signs of terrified soldiers, probably dragging Kuwaiti hostages with them. Where had they all gone? Where were the thousands or tens of thousands who were there only a day or two before? One air pilot, returning from the scene, called it a "turkey shoot." But what happened to the bodies? Did some U.S. commander order them buried? If so, who? And how many were buried? Were the Iraqi soldiers killed in their vehicles as they scrambled north? Or as they sat in one massive traffic jam with no place to hide? Did some run? Were they told to flee across the desert on foot? Were they hit with napalm? Cluster bombs? How many Kuwaiti hostages did the U.S. bombs kill? More, perhaps, than died during the Iraqi occupation of Kuwait? From all appearances what had happened on the road to Basra was a massive slaughter, one of the most one-sided beatings in modern warfare.

Here was the most sophisticated armed military force in history pulverizing a ragtag bunch of virtually defenseless Iraqi soldiers. What happened on the road to Basra that day troubled me deeply; it continues to trouble me long after the war has ended.

Again, within the context of war, some might argue, it made sense. Yet, I *must* wonder. I wonder if any young U.S. officer objected. I wonder if those fleeing soldiers were being hit with all the pent-up vengeance from the U.S. defeat in Vietnam. I wonder if those who found themselves in conscience able to justify this war going in might have had second thoughts coming out. I still do not know how many died during the 43-day war or during the war's last 24 hours. Will the final tallies come to 100,000? 150,000? 200,000?

Violence, we must know, begets violence. History confirms it. How many more Iraqis, Kurds, Iranians, Kuwaitis and others were to die *after* the U.S. bombs stopped falling—but as a direct result of them? Who will suffer most in the next round of the vicious cycle, so intensified by the U.S. involvement? And how much of the violence will return home with the troops who went to the Gulf? How much violence have we and our children already absorbed as a result of the war?

More questions linger. To date, U.S. intelligence has never explained why it so vastly misrepresented the size, strength and will of the Iraqi army. As was the case throughout the six weeks of U.S. bombing, so, too, the four days of ground war ended with many critical questions still unanswered. Among the more important: How could U.S. intelligence, with six months of surveillance and high-resolution photography, not know how many Iraqi troops it had to face? Were there ever, in fact, the 540,000 Iraqi soldiers we had been led to believe? If so, what had happened to them? U.S. military briefers claimed to have cut off most of their escape routes. Were many more killed than the 100,000 the Pentagon begrudgingly estimates lost their lives in the war? Or were there far fewer soldiers to begin with? If so, why did this information not become public before or during the war?

The war remains veiled in mystery, intentionally, so it seems. That's the way the Pentagon seems to want it. Truth, however, has a way of coming to light. Vietnam's My Lai massacre, for example, took more than two years to surface. But if the White House and Pentagon did not seem eager to share with us the dirty details of the war, neither did the U.S. public seem eager to learn about those details. It appeared people wanted to keep their distance from the blood. If, say, 100,000 Iraqi and just over 100 U.S. soldiers died in hostilities, that's a ratio of 1,000 to one. Was it, then, a war? Or was it something else, something more like slaughter, carnage, massacre, butchering? History will tell us.

Sitting in my office on a rainy Kansas City afternoon after a "temporary cease-fire" had been called, I felt *NCR* had something to say, something not being said in the press at the time. None of us in the newsroom felt like joining in with the celebration going on through much of the nation. We felt relief, but we felt a much deeper, profound grief. All I could think of were those bombs and that ghost train, the wreckage of trucks, buses and cars on the road to Basra. That image, for me, came to represent both the slaughter and the veiled mystery that came to be so much a part of the war. We know it all happened, but not how. Our outrage was fed both by what we knew and by what was being kept from us. That rainy afternoon, I pounded out the following words to use as a front-page editorial. It appeared under a headline, "After the Iraqi rout, somber reckonings," and said:

> The post-Vietnam era of so-called U.S. military timidity and national self-doubt ended last week above a highway leading to the Iraqi city of Basra not far from the Euphrates River. It was there, in the alleged cradle of civilization, that U.S., British and French armored divisions, covered by squadrons of U.S. aircraft, rained thousands of tons of explosives on retreating Iraqi troops. Tens of thousands of hemmed-in Iraqi soldiers, it is said, died in the final hours of a conflict reportedly characterized by one U.S. pilot as a "turkey-shoot."
>
> U.S. pride has been restored, U.S. purpose returned to the nation. God help us.

The era of the post-Vietnam War has been replaced by the era of the post-Iraqi rout. It was a rout, never a war. Wars happen when armies face each other. During these military engagements, most Iraqi soldiers died virtually defenselessly in sand bunkers or caught inside buses, tanks or trucks in massive retreat.

This is not to take anything from the U.S. military, which performed, by all accounts, masterfully. It showed itself to be the strongest, most technologically advanced military force in history. Unquestioned U.S. military superiority characterized every aspect of the 43-day conflict.

No modern warfare has ever been more lopsided. U.S. casualties were minimal, for which we are all grateful. Iraqi casualties—military and civilian—by early estimates may run 100,000 or more.

Eventually, we came to live with our defeat in Vietnam. We must now learn to live with our victory in Iraq. It may well be more difficult. Almost certainly more dangerous if our newly emerging arrogance of power is left to run unchecked.

After the parades and celebrations, after the toasts and tears of pride for men and women returning to their families across America, after the last collective sighs of relief have left our lungs, we will be left to face the rest of the world and to explain to our children what our nation did to Iraq in order to free Kuwait. We will be left to ponder, sometime after Saddam Hussein has entered the trash dumps of history in which he belongs, our nation's actions and President Bush's explanation that we went to war "to preserve our way of life." That, too, has been recorded for history. Bush has every right to take credit for the single-mindedness with which he pursued the war. He must one day also take responsibility for what our Air Force, Army and Navy of elephants did to their air force, army and navy of ants.

Bush said he would not hold back. He did not. He crushed Iraq, unleashing bombs upon its cities and third-rate army, purposefully overinflated by U.S. policy-planners to feed U.S. fears and add meaning to what turned out to be a slaughter.

"It would have been very difficult for me to have to kill Iraqis," a Marine said. "They are not really my enemies. It is their leader who is a problem."

Unfortunately, Bush had no such qualms.

Great and powerful nations, understanding their power, show great restraint. What happened in Iraq had nothing to do with what makes a nation great. No, what the United States did to Iraq was a very personal matter having to do with a tragic insecurity deep within President Bush's psyche.

In the end, at incalculable cost to the Iraqi people and to our own nation, this president attempted to prove to us his distorted sense of "manliness." We can celebrate the liberation of Kuwait, but will the means we used to achieve it call down shame upon our nation? Now the celebrations; then the sobering reflections. Historians will judge.

It is ironic that Bush chose that particular spot, neighborhood of the Tigris and Euphrates, to start his "new world order." That, if you believe the old stories, is what God did, too. There's a great danger of hubris hidden here somewhere. (See illustration, page 162.)

Saddam Hussein had to be stopped. But this way? One hundred thousand people, at a minimum, slaughtered? A carnage so vicious, so fiery, that human flesh seemed to have vaporized out of seven miles of charred vehicles without even the blood discoloring

Front page from March 8, 1991 issue of *NCR*.

the sand? A massacre of the bombed innocent, innocence sacrificed so that the wealthy and comfortable may continue on as before?

Saddam Hussein had to be stopped, but this war was wrong as prosecuted. This war was unnecessary. Its motives, suspect on day one, are suspect still—and in time that suspicion will be borne out. Meanwhile, what we have wrought upon Iraq we have visited upon ourselves—but the veils of propaganda and jingoism masquerading as patriotism are the illusion that prevents us from seeing what we *actually* did.   The hollow victory we hold in our hands is only what we *apparently* did—and the victory is an apparition.

We have changed the Middle East and do not know the nature of that change, and we have done it to our own cheers. Ears charmed by the drums of war did not hear that the cheers which followed were a little forced. Those echoed cheers cover the deeper truth that will one day emerge: Though it was a military victory, we have suffered a grave moral defeat.

Appendix

The following is a sampling of prayers, articles and commentaries which appeared in NCR during the Gulf War.

Prayer for Peace

Pope John Paul II

O God of our fathers, great and merciful, Lord of peace and of life, Father of all, you whose designs are for peace and not for affliction, condemn wars and devastate the pride of the violent. You sent your son Jesus to proclaim peace to those near and far, to reunite people of all races and descent into a single family. Hear the unanimous cry of your children, the sorrowful entreaty of all humanity: Never again war, adventure without return; never again war, spiral of struggle and violence; never this war in the Persian Gulf, threat to your creatures in the sky, on earth and in the sea. In communion with Mary, the Mother of Jesus, we continue to implore you: Speak to the hearts of those in charge of the destiny of peoples; stop the logic of retaliation and revenge; suggest with your Spirit new solutions, generous and honorable gestures, spaces for dialogue and patient waiting, which are more fruitful than rushed deadlines of war. Grant to our times days of peace. No war ever again. Amen

Translation courtesy of Catholic News Service. This prayer appeared in the March 1, 1991 issue of NCR.

How Applaud a War That's Like Kicking a Dog?

Joan Chittister

The Saturday morning cartoons are back on TV, uninterrupted and innocent sounding. The new polls are out: Support for the president and the war are up almost 40 points since the war began, to a high of 85 percent.

Things are normal, apparently. So what's the matter with me? Why can't I concentrate on the normal and join the acceptable? Why do I persist in being troubled?

My problem is that I can't get to the state of grace of a knee-jerk liberal. I have to work my way through everything. I'm against war for lots of reasons—moral, ideological, pragmatic—and I'm definitely a nuclear pacifist, but I try to stay real. Evil is a part of life, after all. Is there nothing we would be willing to fight for, to die for, to harm for?

If you accept the notion of war at all, isn't this surely a good one? It is being waged against a known aggressor. It is being fought under terms of military ethics—an assault of military weapons against military installations. And the world is already a safer place because of it: Chemical-weapons plants and nuclear processing facilities, they tell us, were eliminated before the war had barely begun, and with the loss of little or no allied life to do it. The world community, by and large, seems to favor it.

Then why can't I cheer?

Someone wrote once: Better a bad peace than a good war. This one has certainly taught me the truth of that.

There are three problems with this war.

First is the problem of the negative effect of force.

Iraq is a country of 13 million people. Its economy is weak. Its people are poor. Its technology is limited. The United States is 20 times its size and wealth and development. Surely, the United States will "win."

But what will the win say in a world of runaway technology and unequal distribution of resources? Won't the win really say that the great and powerful have the right not to negotiate because they can solve problems the easy way? They can blast everybody else's questions into oblivion, obliterate their opposition, demolish their resistance. Won't the win really say that might does make right, that force is the answer to everything and that the powerful never have to sit down at a table to talk with the powerless?

Or, just as problematic, does being right give anyone the license to destroy the property or destroy the economy or destroy the culture or destroy the institutions of a people that in the end destroys their lives whether they die or not?

The second problem with this war is its capacity for desensitization.

They arc calling this the first full-scale technological war in history. What they mean is that it is inhuman, antiseptic, unreal, remote, "untouched by human hands." Baghdad never sees its enemy and the enemy never sees its victims. The enemy is an unmanned missile launched from carriers hundreds of miles away or a supersonic jet too high or too fast to be spotted.

Neither the crew on the ship nor the crew in the plane ever hears the crash of the bomb or sees the fires they started, or watches the fine, imposing buildings being dynamited out of the heart of the city, or beholds the human faces of the little people who have been caught scurrying in the maelstrom.

Television reporters asked an Air Force colonel who had just returned from one of the 3,000 bombing runs in 14 hours, "What will you do now, Colonel?" and he said, "Well, first I promised to buy my crew coffee. So we'll have breakfast and then we'll get right back to work." Back to killing. Back to work.

And the rest of us watched the war in our living rooms for hours, eating and drinking like we do during the Super Bowl. This war, in other words, is making all of us a little less human. It is really killing everyone.

The third problem with this war is the implications of it.

We have, apparently, given a great deal of thought to this war. The president, newscasters told us, worked on the 15-minute speech announcing the war two weeks before the deadline for starting it. There has not been a word, however, about what we intend to do when it is over.

What shall we do with a devastated country in social, economic and political turmoil? Will we do what we did with Panama and leave its innocent homeless in tents indefinitely?

Will we now provide a standing police force in the Middle East to wage the next war there? And who will pay for a war once estimated at $40 billion and now, just one week later, quickly rebudgeted to $100 billion in a country already too deeply in debt for day care or grants for education?

And how will we deal, in a totally interconnected world, with a frustrated Arab population whose leaders may have given assent to Western forces on Muslim soil but whose people hate the infidel with a passion simple and profound?

The problems are overwhelming. Our win is no win at all, not even if you believe in the ethical conduct of war that, in a world of urban military sites and "collateral damage" and droves of refugees, I do not.

And now, there are more questions than ever.

How is it that, even with advanced technology, more than 7,000 bombing runs were able to destroy no more than 15 percent of the Iraqi Air Force and few of the dreaded Scud missiles?

How is it that we could keep 200,000 troops in Europe for 40 years to contain the Soviet Union, but we didn't have the patience to keep 200,000 troops in Saudi Arabia for five more months to give what was hailed as the most effective international boycott in history even more time to work?

How is it that we never rushed to the rescue of the Cambodians or the Tibetans or the Palestinians on the West Bank, those Arabs without oil, if it is aggression and aggression alone that offends us?

What is it that, if this is truly the war of the international community, the United States has more than 400,000 troops there and the next-largest contingent is the British with only 35,000?

What has happened to the soul of a nation that can applaud a war that is less in the character of a contest and more in the style of beating a child or kicking a dog?

So I'm struggling, torn between the apparent and the real. Is this truly a "just" war? The one we should kill and die and harm the innocent for in the name of justice? For me, the conclusion is getting clearer and clearer: only on the surface.

Benedictine Sister Joan Chittister is writer in residence at Notre Dame University. This article appeared in the February 1, 1991 issue of NCR.

Prejudices Feed Western Intolerance of Islam

Tamara Sonn

At an interfaith dialogue recently in Rochester, N.Y., participants were asked to identify the tradition represented in the following quote: "The covenant between God and humanity requires that we establish a society on earth that reflects the equality we all share in the eyes of God."

The Jews, the Christians and the Muslims present each claimed the sentiment represented their own faiths, though in fact is from the great Pakistani scholar of Islam, Fazlur Rahman, who died in 1987.

The purpose of the exercise was to demonstrate the similarity—indeed, virtual identity—of ethical standards shared by the three "children of Abraham." The three are so similar in belief and even in practice that, as one Hindu scholar put it, their rivalry is nothing more than family jealousy, played out in the context of violence each has shared from the time Joshua fought the first "holy war" at Jericho.

There is ample evidence to support this observation. For centuries Christians persecuted Jews. Anti-Jewish sentiment in Christian Europe culminated in the horrors of Nazi Germany and made necessary the establishment of a state in which Jews felt safe.

Now, in the wake of the Holocaust and the establishment of the state of Israel, Christians have finally begun to face their anti-Judaism; Vatican II addressed the issue directly and issued a clarification designed to expunge the roots of anti-Judaism from Christian scripture. No longer was the account of Jesus' crucifixion in the gospel of John to be interpreted as meaning all Jews are responsible for killing Jesus—only those involved in the event.

There is no scriptural counterpart to the gospel of John regarding Islam. Islam was not born until nearly 600 years after Christ died. Yet Islam has felt the vengeance of Christianity more than once.

The Crusades launched against "the infidels" inspired reams of anti-Islamic propaganda. The Inquisition was convened to rid Spain primarily of its Muslims, as well as of the Jews who thrived in Islamic Spain. And modern European scholars—from Joseph Ernest Renan to Max Weber—have propounded the myth of Islamic inflexibility and anti-intellectualism.

Today, as European Jews fight to make a safe haven for themselves on Palestinian soil; as the Palestinians, quite naturally, fight to maintain their sovereignty, and as the United States leads Europe in a quest to maintain control over Arabs' oil resources, Islam remains vastly misunderstood by the majority of Christians.

Perhaps the most persistent misconceptions Western non-Muslims hold concern perceptions of Islamic intolerance and anti-Christianity, expansionism, violence and fanaticism. Yet just as no Jew recognized Judaism as Christians portrayed it throughout the centuries of Christian intolerance and persecution, no Muslim recognizes Islam as portrayed in these descriptions.

Islam is the simplest of the three Abrahamic faiths. To become Muslim, one need only declare sincerely, "There is no god but *the* God (Allah means *the* God in Arabic, the language of Islamic scripture), and Muhammad is the prophet of God."

This declaration (or witness: *shahada*) is known as the "first pillar" of Islam. According to Islamic belief, this is not a mere verbal or intellectual assent. It carries with it an inevitable change in attitude and behavior. As in Judaism, Islam holds that one cannot truly recognize God's glory, unity, goodness and transcendence without undergoing a fundamental change. True belief will automatically evidence itself in moral behavior.

For this reason, Islam does not require conversion from Judaism or Christianity. From the beginning of Islam in Arabia at the turn of the seventh century, Jews and Christians have been known as "people of the book." "The book" is true scripture, revealed through the entire line of prophets from Abraham, through Moses and Jesus, and up to Prophet Muhammad.

Jews and Christians have all received true revelation. Some members of each community have tampered with the revelation so as to allow for such deviation as the belief that salvation was meant only for a chosen race, or that Jesus is divine and therefore able to achieve human salvation.

Islam believes the great Prophet Jesus came to correct the first misinterpretation; Jesus' message was that salvation was meant for all people, regardless of the condition of their birth. What is more, Jesus confirmed the covenant of Abraham, teaching that salvation was not achievable through mere ritual or legalism. The true route to salvation lay in the two greatest commandments: Love God and love your neighbors as you love yourselves.

Yet, according to Islam, some of Jesus' followers contravened that teaching. In their excessive zeal, they deified Jesus and thus compromised the belief in the one God with whom the covenant was made. This, in turn, undermined the greatest commandments Jesus taught, by claiming salvation could be achieved vicariously, through someone else's sacrifice. In Islam, salvation can be achieved solely through moral behavior commitment to the one God will produce—through commitment to the two greatest commandments.

Still, Islam gives both Jews and Christians special status. As people of the book, they are not required to declare Islam. Provided they behave morally and do not interfere with Islamic practice, they are "protected peoples" in the Islamic world.

With rare exceptions, they were never subjected to prejudicial behavior. They were always allowed their own houses of worship, they own schools, their own courts. They only had to pay a special tax, in lieu of the poor-tax they would have paid if they had been Muslim.

As is well known, the "golden age" of Judaism was enjoyed in Islamic Spain. When the Inquisition began and Spanish Jews took refuge in other Islamic lands, the Islamic leader welcomed them, saying, "Spain's loss is my gain."

Forced conversion is expressly forbidden in the Islamic holy book, the Qur'an. (Today, only in Saudi Arabia—the state the United States is pledged to defend at the expense of war—are non-Muslims banned from worshiping openly in the community.)

The other four "pillars" of Islam are all designed to remind Muslims of their commitment to God's covenant—the call for social justice: regular daily prayer (*salat*), performed at dawn, mid-morning, noon, midafternoon and evening; giving one's wealth to support the poor (*zakat*); fasting from sunrise to sunset (the "fourth pillar," *sawm*) during the holy month of Ramadan; and the annual pilgrimage to Mecca, to be performed at least once a lifetime if one is physically and financially able.

Commitment to social justice makes one Muslim, and, according to Islamic teaching, only when all people work for the goal of justice and equality will it be achieved. Indeed, the great Islamic legist Ibn Taymiyya, who died in 1328, claimed the social teaching of the Qur'an could be summarized on one verse from the book, "Prescribe good and proscribe evil."

In this context, Muslims find Western perceptions of Islamic extremism and fanaticism sadly ironic. At the turn of the 20th century, the Islamic world was for the most part under colonial control. Although official control of the Middle East and parts of North Africa was not granted until the end of World War I, effective control had been achieved much earlier, by France, Britain and Italy.

When Muslims began to call for revival of the Islamic spirit to oust colonial rulers, their self-criticism centered on laxity, fatalism and excessive tolerance bordering on apathy. How else could Christians have taken control of Syria, Iraq, Egypt, Libya and other lands?

Yet as they did so, the West seemed to dredge up its old prejudices from the days of the Crusades and the Inquisition to justify its continued control.

It seems that now is the time for Christianity to transcend these prejudices toward Islam, as it has attempted to do with its prejudice against Judaism. If we are all to teach human equality, when will we begin to practice it?

Tamara Sonn is director of the international studies program at St. John Fisher College, Rochester, N.Y. This article appeared in the special supplement, "A Primer: Christianity meets Islam," which accompanied the February 8, 1991 issue of NCR.

A Prayer Offered for a 'Long' Gulf War

William R. Callahan

As the war with Iraq became inevitable, I prayed to God that it be brief. But as the censored news delivered by enthusiasts for war began its controlled flow, I changed my prayer. I began praying for a "long" war.

I hate war. Its wasteful weaponry and military structures consume the poor of the earth, eat the food of the children and train good human beings to become instruments of death. War is contrary to the way of Jesus.

But a short war with Iraq threatens dire consequences for our earth and for the United States. If the massive air bombardment ends the war in a few days, the political and military establishment of the United States and its allies will be jubilant.

Apart from a few planes shot down and minimal casualties, the technology of war will be proved triumphant. We "kicked ass" without being bloodied in return. Iraqis did the dying. Iraqi parents will do the wailing.

Americans will relax and rejoice and go back to another Super Bowl, awed by the planning and prowess of our military and the resolve of our triumphant president and compliant Congress. To the swift crushing of Panama will be added the dramatic smashing of Iraq.

The military/industrial complex and their high-tech weapons will be vindicated for the future. The military budget will be untouchable. Military planners and political leaders who urged the war will celebrate appropriations to replace the "glorious" war materials to guard against future "Iraqs." War will have triumphed.

No, it is better that we experience a long war. Let it be long enough for casualties to be shared and mount for all the nations involved.

If Iraq survives long enough, then U.S. enthusiasm for war will start to cool. High-tech weapons will lose their glitter. Media control and military censorship will start to crumble. The war's enthusiasts will grow hoarse. As U.S. bodies begin to return in "human remains pouches," protests will mobilize and mount.

Our nation will start to hear the weeping parents, the widowed spouses and the children mourning their parents. The collective hysteria of patriotism whipped up by political leaders and tamed media, who only interview military families and parrot military briefings, will collapse. The U.S. people and other nations will listen again to the pain of their sisters and brothers faced with the agonies, stupidity, immorality and futility of war.

If only the war can last long enough, then perhaps it will present us a healing gift. Just as Vietnam, like a bloody leech, sucked out the war lust of an earlier generation, the suffering of this war will drain the infectious climate of war in our generation. Then, in God's mysterious paradox, healing will flow from violence, and suffering will redeem the folly of this struggle.

Jesuit Father William R. Callahan is codirector of the Quixote Center, based in Mt. Rainier, Md. This article appeared in the February 15, 1991 issue of NCR.

War Incurs for U.S. a Profound Outside Odium

Rosemary Radford Ruether

For the first two weeks of the U.S. bombing of Iraq I was in India. On the Jan. 15 "deadline," I was lecturing in the Gurukul Theological Seminary in Madras. The class took a moment to pray that good sense would prevail and that the United States and its allies would not pursue the announced military course.

The war analysis in India newspapers provided a different context from what U.S. Americans were experiencing in the media reporting of the war back home. The Indian government, while it condemned Hussein's invasion of Kuwait, supported a negotiated solution, not military force.

Although most Hindu or Christian Indians do not admire Hussein, they see him more as a fool than an evil genius, someone who was trapped into a war of destruction of his country by an intransigent American stance that allowed him no "honorable" means of negotiation but demanded unconditional surrender.

By contrast, for the Muslim communities of India and Pakistan, the American war has made Hussein a hero. As we approached the area of the great 16th-century Moghul mosque in Delhi, we saw that large posters of a smiling Hussein were being hawked on the steps. We became instant "Canadians," if asked.

Even though most Indian papers are heavily dependent on Washington, D.C., for their international news, and hence for news of the Gulf war, the analysis of the war was totally different from that of the mainline American news media. Disgust and cynicism toward Bush's self-righteous rhetoric of a moral crusade was general, and horror at the excessive violence of the American air war grew daily.

M.S. Ajwani, editorialist in the Delhi *Hindustan Times*, summed up the general view of the Indians in these words: "The war is certainly not for saving democracy or a fight against dictatorship. All this is nonsense. They have no such interest. There is no such interest. Their interest is in oil. As Kissinger put it very picturesquely: 'to have assured supplies and at an acceptable price.' Now, this is the real game."

For Ajwani, the roots of the war lie in British and American hegemonic control over Arab oil, which used wealthy emirs and sheiks to assure such control. These emirs and sheiks live in extravagant luxury at the expense of the vast majority of Arabs who have no oil and who never see any of the benefits of oil profits. Indeed, these profits are mainly plowed into the Western European and American economies through purchasing arms and investing in Western banks and businesses.

The war is seen to be about maintaining and securing the hegemonic control, by destroying the one Arab country, militarily and economically, that was beginning to challenge this control. This judgment is quite separate from whether Saddam Hussein is a just ruler of his own people.

Nevertheless, as an Arab leader, he was seeking to redress an unjust Western control of Arab resources by Western interests. This is seen as compelling the sympathy of Asian people, who also see themselves as victims of this hegemonic Western control over their resources.

Since returning from India at the end of January, I have been startled by the total lack of such critical analysis in U.S. papers and image media, with the exception of small newspapers and journals "on the left." On the contrary, the mainstream American media seem totally captured and controlled by righteous self-congratulation and infatuated with our own capacity for technological violence. The air war, solely from the American side, has been turned into a media sporting event, filtered through a blanket denial of civilian casualties.

I find myself sickened by newspaper and TV reporting of the war. The other day I overheard one newscaster announce, "Today, American bombing sorties topped 50,000!" The excited tone was that of a sportscaster announcing the breaking of a record by our "team."

My mind flashed back to discussions in the late 1940s about how Europe went fascist and whether "it could happen here." We are seeing the beginnings of how it could "happen here." When the media suspend critical judgment and hand themselves over to news control by the military, the crucial step has been taken toward fascism.

It is important for Americans to realize they are increasingly living in a closed society, isolated from the vast majority of world opinion. We delude ourselves if we think that Asians, Africans, even most Europeans support our choice of overwhelming military force to solve a problem that demanded patience and negotiation.

We also delude ourselves if we think that support by the Arab leaders in power in Egypt, Saudi Arabia, much less Syria, means that most of the "Arab world" is on our side. Rather, it is these Arab leaders who are isolated from the Arab people and they will undoubtedly pay the price for this isolation in time.

With every bomb rained on the Iraqi people, the United States loses moral credibility in most of the world and brings upon itself profound odium, not only among Arabs, but also among Asians and Africans. As Ajwani put it in the conclusion of his Jan. 27 editorial, "Americans will find it increasingly hard to dominate the region, regardless of the outcome of the war. Even if Saddam is removed from the scene, his ghost will haunt the Americans in West Asia to no end."

Rosemary Radford Ruether is a professor of theology at Garrett-Evangelical Theological Seminary, Evanston, Ill. This article appeared in the March 1, 1991 issue of NCR.

Jail Makes War Protest Significant

Jeff Dietrich

"Hey man, what they give you?"

Although we share the same jail cell, packed in like sardines, our situations are as different as our physical appearances. Big Jake has mountains of tight, black muscle. Despite being wrapped in leg irons, he is unsubdued. Even the normally rude guards are deferential in his presence. I, on the other hand, am pitifully diminutive and painfully white in this sea of pulchritude and color.

"They're holding me in lieu of $10,000 bail," I lie, trying to sound as tough as my 140-pound frame will allow.

"Ah, that ain't nothing. Willie here, he's got a million-dollar bail."

How could I admit to these men, facing 10 or 20 years or even life, that upon the payment of a single dollar I could be on the streets again. They already think all seven of us protesters border on the mentally deficient. While it was "pretty cool" to pour 30 gallons of oil and two pints of blood on the steps of the Federal Building to protest the war, we never should have gotten ourselves arrested.

"That was one messed-up deal. You should've run like hell after you dumped that oil," said Jake. "You ain't gonna do shit for your cause in here."

Oddy enough, that was essentially, though less colorfully, what Judge Reichmann had said as well. In setting our bail at one dollar rather than the $10,000 the prosecution had asked for, Reichmann had hoped we would choose to buy our freedom rather than burden his conscience by forcing him to put us in jail—a waste of our time. He even went so far as to outline for us an effective program of public outreach: "Speak on campuses, get on radio talk shows, write letters to Congress, but don't go to jail."

But to buy our way out of jail, even for a dollar, robs our actions of any possible significance they might have. Talk is cheap, but authentic freedom, which is always the response to truth, is paid for in the currency of conviction. Cheap freedom, like cheap grace, is bereft of all substance and conviction.

It was, and remains, our hope that some conscience may indeed be burdened by our presence in jail. It is not our desire to merely add our words to the great storm of words about the war that now pours down upon the nation. Reporters officials, experts, protesters, talk-show hosts are all finally, as Shakespeare said, a sound and a fury.

Our desire is that we might speak words with content and gravity. Our soldiers have invested their lives in words; they are prepared to give the final payment, the sacrifice that makes those words effective. If we have heard a different word, should we not likewise be prepared to make a sacrifice to give significance to that word?

Significance is different from effectiveness. Significance is a quality of being, while effectiveness is a function of doing. Significance is simply a sign of something greater, while effectiveness is winning, accomplishing, succeeding.

War is perhaps the most effective of all human enterprises, at least for the victor. Yet, who can ever remember why we fought the Mexican-American War? Who remembers the generals or even the president who led us? Who remembers the noble sentiments, the sacred words that inspired that conflict?

No one remembers. And yet the entire world remembers the thin, gangly man with the intense eyes and unkempt hair who spent a single night in the Concord jail because he refused to pay even one dollar to finance the conflict.

Who will remember, a hundred years hence, the noble sentiments and sacred words that inspire the current conflict? Who will remember the generals and the president who now lead us? No doubt they will be effective, but will they be significant? Will the word they speak point to something greater? Will it last through time and continue to validate the sacrifice of so many?

On the other hand, those of us who languish in jail are not effective. We will not mobilize vast armies of supporters. Our word will not be spoken to the multitudes. We cannot be heard amid the sound and the fury of wartime. But one must wonder to whom history will give the last word.

We have heard this word in our hearts that will not be silent. We have attempted to invest the word with the gravity of at least some portion of our lives. We offer it as a meagre sacrifice with the hope that some significance might remain through time.

Jeff Deitrich is a member of the Catholic Worker community in Los Angeles. This article appeared in the March 1, 1991 issue of NCR.

There Must Also Be Those Who See Tragedy

James K. Healy

Surely, there is no one present this morning who does not grieve with the mothers and fathers, the spouses, the sisters and brothers and children of those tragic fallen few of our citizens who died in the Gulf conflict.

We are of one great heart in our tremendous relief, our euphoria, that what we feared would be such a long and bloody conflict has, for us, been so relatively brief and painless. We can be sure the unanimous mind of the American people is ours, and ours is theirs.

But there must be a people somewhere who mourn and grieve in the depths of their being for the wailing women of Iraq. There must be a people other than the Iraqis themselves who feel in the midst of this (Western) triumph, a deep and penetrating sense of tragedy, that it should have come to this, that so many should have died.

There has to be among the people, a chosen people who feel at the very least, uncomfortable, and perhaps even irate, that it took so long to hear even speculative figures about how many Iraqi soldiers died in this terrible conflict.

There must be a people who will demand an accounting, and soon, that the full price paid by our enemies be known to all of those who would savor the triumph.

There must be a people who (surveying this Middle East region) feel, too, for the Palestinian people. There must be a people whose prayers of gratitude that *our* war is over are matched by passionate prayers of pleading with God that the Palestinians might at last have a place they can call home, and their own. There must be a people.

183

There must be those who see through the ugly faces as portrayed by our media, let us say with some accuracy, our political propaganda, who see beyond the caricaturized face of an Arafat or the gruesome face of Saddam Hussein, who see a people troubled, a people grieving, a people needing understanding, a people crying out for what will never make common sense: that there be common cause among all the peoples of the earth, knowing we're all one family. There must be such a people.

My sisters and brothers, I suggest to you this morning that these people, this strange and contradictory people, a stumbling block in the eyes of their neighbors, is *this* people: that *we* are these people.

Paul said it to the Corinthians: We preach a Christ crucified, we talk about a Lord who gets humiliated, we talk about a triumph that is the world's most colossal defeat. Paul said we preach a message to the Jews that, as they ask for signs and proofs, will be sheer folly; a message to the Greeks—who prided themselves on their rationality, their logic, their ability to reason out everything—which will be just a stumbling block.

Yet, that is the Jesus we preach.

The above is excerpted from a homily Father James Healy delivered at Queen of Peace Church, Arlington, Va., March 3. It appeared in the March 15, 1991 issue of NCR.

War Poetry Sets Same Challenge as Bodies: What Does War Mean?

Michael J. Farrell

There's something about war that loves a poem. The intensity, perhaps, demands the density of poetry. Most of the great epics thunder with war. Often, the wars were far from great until the poems retroactively made them so, and often the ultimate outcome of a war depended on the poem, the people not won by force but only, centuries later, when the songs sank deep enough into the human core.

Thus, the remark attributed to Thomas Jefferson (among others), "Let others write a nation's laws if I could write its songs," could usefully be adjusted to, "Let others pulverize a nation's cities if I could write its songs." We have probably blown our chances to write Iraq's.

A timely new book, *Articles of War: A Collection of American Poetry about World War II*, edited by Leon Stokesbury (University of Arkansas Press, 229 pages, $24.95), helps explain how war and poetry, after walking so long hand in hand, finally diverged in World War I and were at each other's throats in World War II. Given the fervent patriotic spirit that stokes our current war, it will be intriguing to see what kind of Muse will come trailing.

England's Rupert Brooke offers a good example of where the Muse came in—the old-fashioned poetic sanctification of war:

If I should die, think only this of me:
That there's some corner of a foreign field
That is for ever England. . . .

Probably never did so many good poets go to war as to World War I, which quickly knocked the daylights out of the poets and the romance out of poetry. The glory wrung from it, the poetry

185

was banal, matter-of-fact, then weary, then angry. Wrote Siegfried Sassoon:

> "Good morning, good morning!" the general said
> When we met him last week on our way to the line.
> Now the soldiers he smiled at are most of 'em dead,
> And we're cursing his staff for incompetent swine.

And Arthur Graeme West:

> Next was a bunch of half a dozen men
> All blown to bits, an archipelago
> Of corrupt fragments. . . .

And Sassoon has a word for the fervent patriotism of those who wave flags and holler for "our boys" whom, for one reason or another, they have neglected to join in the Arab sands:

> You smug-faced crowds with kindling eye
> Who cheer when soldier lads march by,
> Sneak home and pray you'll never know
> The hell where youth and laughter go.

These developments set the aspiring poets of World War II a problem. By 1943, British poet Keith Douglas wrote, "In the fourth year of this war we have not a single poet who seems likely to be an impressive commentator on it." The reason given was that all the best words and expressions for anger, stupidity, pain, futility had been used up. "Hell cannot be let loose twice," observed Douglas.

Thus, writes Paul Fussell in an introduction to *Articles of War*, "the mode of Second War poetry represents a general skepticism about the former languages of glory and sacrifice and patriotism. Sick of the inflated idiom of official morale-boosting tub-thumping and all the slynesses of wartime publicity and advertising, the poets now preferred to speak in wry understatement. . . . Finding language so greatly abused in public, some poets could barely bring themselves to deploy it in private."

In this collection, nevertheless, some well-known poets stand up and demand attention. For example, Marianne Moore:

Hate-hardened heart, O heart of iron,
    iron is iron till it is rust.
There never was a war that was
    not inward: I must
fight till I have conquered in myself what
    causes war. . . .

"The young dead soldiers do not speak," begins Archibald MacLeish. Yet, the dead soldiers are heard. "They say: We leave you our deaths. Give them their meaning." . . .

Most of the poets, dejected or cynical, come bearing less moral ballast than the above. John Ciardi begins one: "Tibia, tarsel, skull, and shin:/Bones come out where the guns go in."

Howard Nemerov's "The War in the Air" is even more appropriate this month than half a century ago:

For a saving grace, we didn't see our dead,
Who rarely bothered coming home to die
But simply stayed away out there
In the clean war, the war in the air.

But, lest the romance creep back, Nemerov soon returns to the safer haven of banality. Does he hate Hitler? a poem asks. Hell, no, he has no time or energy for that. But Wing Commander Briggs and the group captain et al, now that's different—"those bastards were bastards in your daily life."

There are poems of awful brutality, of futility and stupidity. But there remains a disconcerting paradox. If the poetry is good— and in this book it is—it somehow ennobles war by even dealing with its worst horrors.

There are poems about terrible executions, but somehow a great poet writing about even a horrible death seems to make it in a way worthwhile to have died, now that the pain is over, to be remembered by such a poet whose subsequent attention bestows a balm or benediction on the life and death. Thus, in an insidious twist, even antiwar poetry can lift war up.

By contrast, the following prose passage from *Soldiers: A History of Men in Battle* (Viking, 1985), all unadorned, denies war the poetic wrapping, puts no fancy words or sentiments between us and the reality:

> As contact with the enemy draws nearer, anticipation sharpens into fear. Its physical effects are striking. The heart beats rapidly, the face shines with sweat and the mouth grows dry—so dry that men often emerge from battle with blackened mouths and chapped lips. The jaws gape or the teeth chatter, and in an effort to control himself a man may clench his jaw so tightly that it will ache for days afterwards. Many lose control of their bladder or their bowels. Nearly a quarter of the soldiers of an American division interviewed in the South Pacific admitted that they had fouled themselves, and the spectacle of soldiers urgently urinating just before they go into action is as old as battle itself.

And then there are those who come home from war mad. Recent literature on the subject indicates that, because of more expert treatment, the numbers of the insane are down in recent wars. Yet, it's true that, while those who voted for this present war go on with their political and other careers, men and women, here and in Iraq, will spend the rest of their lives staring at walls. . . .

Meanwhile, it's hard to say what kind of poetry the Gulf War will bring.

Michael J. Farrell is NCR's senior editor. This article appeared in the March 1, 1991 issue of NCR.

Index